D1135639

Countryside

KITCHEN

FARM ★ FOOD ★ FORK

First published in Great Britain by

National Farmers' Union

Agriculture House

Stoneleigh Park

Stoneleigh

Warwickshire CV8 2TZ

Copyright © NFU 2017

The right of the NFU to be identified as the author of this work has been asserted in accordance with the Copyright, Designs and Patents Act 1988. All rights reserved. No part of this publication may be reproduced or transmitted in any form or by any means, electronic or mechanical, including photocopy, recording or any information storage and retrieval system, without the prior written permission of the publisher, nor by way of trade or otherwise shall be lent, re-sold, hired out or otherwise circulated without the publisher's prior consent in any form of binding or cover other than that in which it is published and without a similar condition including this condition being imposed on the subsequent purchaser.

ISBN 978-1-9998061-0-1

Printed and bound in the UK
by CLOC Limited
Unit 10 Milmead Industrial Centre
London N17 9QU

CONTRIBUTORS

Head of Publishing: Mike Carr

Head of Communications: Sharon Hockley

Group Design Manager: Chris Warren

Designers: Toby Lea and Darren Ryley

Art Editor: Rachel Warner

Recipe Editor and Indexer: Michéle Moody

Production Manager: Heather Lewis

Membership and Marketing Adviser: Mandy Frisby

Catering Manager: Pauline Pentland

Catering Assistants: Surrinder Hothi and Daniel Batchelor

Departmental Administrator: Jayne Pearson

Photography:

Adam Fradgley, Tim Scrivener, Howard Barlow, Toby Lea, John Cottle, Clive Streeter, Jane Russell, Cotswold Farm Park © StockFood, The Food Media Agency

Additional thanks to Simon Ashby, Sarah Burley-Jukes, Helen Cotterill, Amy Gray, Lisa Gudge, Chris Pryke, Alex Lacey, Orla McIlduff, Tom Sales, Tracey Saunders, Martin Stanhope and Jessica Stobart

The National Farmers' Union is the voice of British farming. It works to protect and shape a productive, profitable and progressive future for British food and farming.

**For further information go to
www.nfuonline.com**

NFU Countryside is a membership organisation that celebrates all that's great about the British countryside. Our key purpose is to stress that the British countryside is a living, working environment.

**For further information go to
www.countrysideonline.co.uk**

INTRODUCTION

Adam Henson

Where would we be without great British food? From tasty lamb grown on our beautiful grassy hills and mountains, to the fruit and wheat from our more productive regions with fertile soils and a favourable climate. Iconic beef, nutritious dairy, chicken, eggs – not forgetting home-grown sugar beet; we have it all.

British farmers produce some of the most delicious and diverse food to some of the highest, ethical and sustainable standards in the world. And thanks to our four unique seasons, the food we harvest differs month by month, bringing to our plates a colourful palate of taste sensations.

It's no wonder the UK's food culture is thriving. The past decade has seen the emergence of hundreds of delis, farmers' markets, farm shops and food festivals across the country. People more than ever want to learn where their food comes from. A passion for cooking has been reignited with TV chef-inspired dishes using local produce, rather than food that's been air-freighted across the world from an unknown source.

Shoppers want to know more about the people behind the food on their plate. I strongly believe it's essential we convey our personalities, passions and ethos as farmers through books, TV programmes, social media or even via the label on a carton of milk, so we can improve and strengthen this vital connection between farmer and you, our customer. In this era, more than most in fact, communication is everything and we have a very positive story to share.

I am immensely proud of my farming heritage; a feeling shared by every farmer and grower across the land. We are proud to be part of a food-producing powerhouse that shapes our beautiful, diverse countryside, plays a leading role in animal welfare standards, and is the backbone of rural communities. More than that, food and farming contributes more than £100 billion to the national economy and provides jobs for around four million people. Everyone is touched by this innovative sector, from the milk in their tea, to the ingredients for their favourite dish – but people have become disconnected with how their food is produced and the best time to buy it in season. And that is what this recipe book is all about.

Britain is currently 61% self-sufficient in food – but we can do more. And you, as a shopper, have immense power and a huge role to play. The more that shoppers request – and buy – British food from their supermarkets and independent retailers, the better the chance of an outlet for the farmers who produce this food. And a thriving, food-producing farming sector is good for our nation's wealth and health.

So my message to you is simple. Use this recipe book to help reconnect with the great British seasons in all their glory, keep buying and cooking seasonal, local and British food dishes and above all celebrate all that's great about British food and farming.

Cook the food...

6

MEET the FARMERS

Food and farming contributes more than

£100 billion

to the nation's coffers

It provides jobs for more than

THREE million PEOPLE

There are around

140,000 family farming BUSINESSES

of all shapes and sizes in the UK

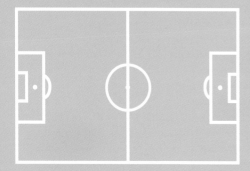

The wildflower meadows and habitats created by farmers for wildlife would cover

more than 10,000 FOOTBALL PITCHES

British farmers have some of the

HIGHEST standards

of animal welfare in the world

1 in 3 FARMS

produces or uses renewable energy helping to sustain a cleaner, greener planet

ABOUT THIS BOOK

Here at NFU and NFU Countryside we are hugely passionate about great British food and the farmers and growers whose ingenuity, knowledge and determination produces and delivers that food from farm to plate. So much so we want to share with you this incredible journey.

Welcome to *Countryside Kitchen: Farm Food Fork*. A new and exciting recipe book that is packed full of great tasting dishes, aimed at those new to cooking as well as those celebrity chefs in the making.

Countryside Kitchen is the first to celebrate our British farmers and growers who work in all weathers across our diverse and iconic landscape to produce fantastic food for our plates.

As anyone who has tried to grow any type of food at home will appreciate, modern food production on the scale needed to feed a growing nation must be, and is, a very highly skilled, immensely innovative area.

The team here has been inspired by the amazing farmers and growers that you will meet in the following pages; their passion, dedication and good humour when faced with the trials and tribulations associated with every-day farming. These are the same people who help to grow and rear the fantastic ingredients listed in this book and we hope that you enjoy meeting them as much as we have.

Page after page, this recipe book will help you to navigate the four stunning British seasons so you can find which home-grown foods are abundantly available and when, meaning you can buy great British season food, create culinary delights and celebrate that incredible journey from farm to fork.

British farming is incredibly important to us as a nation. Culturally and historically our country has been shaped by farming. And our beautiful, iconic landscape continues to be formed by those working the land.

Thank you to each and every one of you who has contributed to this collection of recipes and farmer stories, and to those who continue to provide the food for our plates.

WINTER

Dark nights make way for comforting casseroles
and decadent dishes fit for festive sparkle

Parsnip and GINGER SOUP

Serves: 4 // Preparation time: 10 minutes // Cooking time: 35 minutes

INGREDIENTS

2 tbsp vegetable oil
1 large onion, chopped
750g parsnips
1 clove garlic, chopped
2cm piece root ginger, peeled
   and chopped
1.15 litres vegetable stock
3 tbsp crème fraîche
chopped parsley and a little
   ground paprika to serve

METHOD

1. Heat the oil in a large pan, add
   the onion and sauté for 3–4
   minutes or until pale golden.

2. Meanwhile, wash the parsnips,
   trim the ends and chop them
   into even sized chunks.

3. Add the parsnips to the pan
   along with the garlic and ginger,
   sauté for 2 minutes, stirring.

4. Pour in the stock and add a little
   seasoning. Bring to the boil, cover
   and simmer for 20–25 minutes or
   until the parsnips are tender.

5. Use a stick blender to purée the
   soup until it is nice and smooth.

6. Add the crème fraîche and taste for
   seasoning. Serve hot in bowls, sprinkled
   with a little parsley or paprika.

LEEK and Stilton SOUP

Serves: 6 // Preparation time: 30 minutes // Cooking time: 45 minutes

INGREDIENTS

8 leeks, trimmed, washed
   and finely chopped in
   a food processor
2 sticks of celery, roughly
   chopped, with a few
   strips left for garnishing
50g butter
1 tbsp light and mild olive oil
1 large baking potato,
   peeled and diced
1.75 litres vegetable stock
150ml single cream
225g Stilton cheese, crumbled
generous seasoning of
   sea salt and ground
   black pepper to taste

METHOD

1. Gently sweat the chopped leek
   and celery in the butter and olive
   oil for 5 minutes to soften.

2. Add the diced potato and stock.
   Bring to a gentle simmer. Cover
   and cook for 30 minutes.

3. Blend in batches in a food processor
   with the single cream, Stilton and
   seasonings to a coarse consistency.

4. Serve topped with strips of cooked
   leek, and with warm crusty
   granary bread on the side.

TOP TIP Look for the Red Tractor logo when shopping for your
ingredients to ensure you are buying quality British produce.

15

Beef and Chutney
TOASTIES

Serves: 2 // Preparation time: 10 minutes // Cooking time: 10 minutes

INGREDIENTS

1 tbsp rapeseed or olive oil
1 small onion, peeled
   and sliced
1 tbsp fresh thyme leaves
2 lean thinly cut beef steaks
salt and freshly ground
   black pepper
2 tbsp Dijon or
   wholegrain mustard
3 tbsp light or reduced
   calorie mayonnaise
4 slices ciabatta bread
50–75g vintage Cheddar
   cheese, sliced
2 tbsp prepared onion chutney
rocket leaves to garnish

METHOD

1. Heat half the oil in a non-stick
   frying or griddle pan.

2. Add the onion and thyme and cook
   over a low heat for 3–4 minutes
   until the onions are soft. Transfer
   to a small bowl and set aside.

3. Season the beef and cook for 1–2 minutes
   on each side until brown then
   set aside.

4. In a small bowl mix the mustard and
   mayonnaise together and spread over the
   two bread slices. Top with the cheese and
   cook under a preheated grill for
   1–2 minutes until the cheese has melted.

5. Add the chutney, rocket leaves, steaks
   and onions then sandwich together
   with the remaining two bread slices.

6. Serve with chunky chips and
   a side salad.

TOP TIP If you fancy making your own chutney,
why not try the recipe on p.59.

The Timmis Family

The Timmis family own a mixed farm in Baschurch,
near Shrewsbury, and it has been in the family
since 1919, so a big party is imminent!

Mike and Hazel Timmis and their three daughters – Emma, Melissa and Elaine – and their respective husbands – Russell, Dan and Terry – run the family farm, with help from Nana. Who could run a farm without a Nana, tasting new products and doing the ironing?

They grow wheat, barley, oats and oil seed rape and look after a lovely range of animals: Hereford beef cattle, Gloucester Old Spot pigs, Shropshire sheep and Warren chickens – all free range – alongside polo ponies.

"This is a way of life, not a job," says Elaine. "It is not all plain sailing but I wouldn't change it for the world. I love being able to get up in the morning and think what can I improve today, what new things would I like to do? To look out on the beautiful scenery makes me realise how lucky I am to be here. Having family around makes all the difference with a support structure there and everyone seeing things in a different way, offering different ideas and talents."

This particular summer has been really busy for the Timmis family. They launched a polo club and bought a marquee at the beginning of the year that they hire out for weddings and events, so there is always something going on. A typical day

for Elaine is making sure everything is OK in the farm shop, filling in for anyone who is away or on holiday. She continues: "One day I might be cooking breakfasts, the next I might be making sausages. If there is an event on at the weekend, I will be making sure everything has been ordered or booked. I do the accounts, ordering – everything really. Many farms diversify into different businesses, in the main to support the farming side of things. Farming is vulnerable to lots of pressures, including the weather, markets and prices, so spreading the business risk makes sense and helps us to ensure the farm will be viable for the next 100 years.

"We all have trouble saying no to new ideas, which is why in the past 12 years we have built a new farm, opened a farm shop, built a bigger farm shop, added on a tea room, extended the cattle sheds added to make room for more cows to provide for the farm shop, put solar panels on the shed roofs and started up a polo club. And there are still many more ideas in the pipeline."

It is hardly surprising that her favourite British dish has to be a family Sunday lunch of roast beef, made, of course, from their Hereford beef cattle, in the family also since 1919.

One Pot Potato
and PORK CHILLI

Serves: 4 // Preparation time: 5 minutes // Cooking time: 30 minutes

INGREDIENTS

1 tbsp oil
500g diced pork leg
1 yellow pepper, diced
800g potatoes, diced
410g can kidney beans,
    drained and rinsed
500g jar sauce for
    chilli con carne

METHOD

1. Heat the oil in a large saucepan and fry the pork and pepper for 5 minutes.

2. Add the potatoes, kidney beans and chilli con carne sauce. Wash the jar out with a little water and add to the pan.

3. Bring to the boil, cover and simmer for 25 minutes or until the potatoes and pork are cooked throughout. Serve immediately.

TOP TIP For vegetarians replace the pork with a meat alternative such as diced Quorn, adding it to the pan for the last 5 minutes.

Tasty chicken and HAM PIE

Serves: 4–6 // Preparation and cooking time: 1 hour 45 minutes

INGREDIENTS

- 1 whole chicken and 6 boned thighs
- 1 slice gammon
- 1 large leek, finely chopped
- 75g butter
- 3 level tbsp plain flour
- 600ml milk
- 150ml (approx.) strong chicken stock (from poaching)
- 2 tbsp mascarpone
- 1 pack ready-rolled puff pastry
- 1 egg, whisked

METHOD

1. Roast the whole chicken and poach the thighs in chicken stock until cooked.

2. Take all the chicken off the bone and cut into chunky uneven pieces.

3. Cut the gammon slice into strips and dry fry or oven cook until lightly cooked.

4. Sweat the leeks in butter – but do not let them colour.

5. Add 75g butter.

6. Add the flour and gently cook for 1 minute.

7. Gradually add the milk and stir until thickened.

8. Add the chicken stock that the thighs were cooked in and stir until thickened.

9. Stir in the mascarpone, chicken and ham, then leave in the pie dish to cool.

10. Set the oven again to 180°C/fan 160°C/350°F/ gas mark 4.

11. Cut the puff pastry to fit the pie dish. Use any trimmings to attach to the lip of the dish with water.

12. Crimp edges and then brush with the egg.

13. Bake for 15 minutes, then reduce to 160°C for a further 30 minutes.

TOP TIP Look for the Red Tractor logo when shopping for your ingredients to ensure you are buying quality British produce.

Roast Sirloin OF BEEF

WITH CHESTNUT & CHIVE BUTTER, CARAMELISED PARSNIPS AND LEEKS

Serves: 8 // Preparation time: 10 minutes

INGREDIENTS

For the chestnut and chive butter

75g unsalted butter, softened
75g can unsweetened chestnut purée
grated zest 2 oranges
1 tsp ground cinnamon
2 tbsp freshly chopped chives

1.3–1.8kg lean sirloin, fore rib or topside joint
salt and freshly milled black pepper
900g leeks, topped, tailed and cut in half lengthways
900g medium parsnips, peeled and cut in half lengthways
4 tbsp sherry vinegar

For the red wine gravy

25g plain flour
450ml hot beef stock
300ml full bodied red wine

METHOD

1. Preheat the oven to 180–190°C/fan 160–170°C/350–375°F/gas mark 4–5.

2. Prepare the chestnut and chive butter: in a small bowl mix together the butter, chestnut purée, orange zest, cinnamon and chives.

3. Place the joint on a chopping board, score the skin, season on both sides and spread generously with the chestnut butter. Place any remaining butter in cling film, mould into a sausage shape and freeze for up to 2 months.

4. Transfer the joint to a metal rack in a large non-stick roasting tin and open roast for the preferred, calculated cooking time, basting occasionally with any meat juices. Cover with foil if browning too quickly.

5. About 45 minutes before the end of the cooking time, remove the joint and rack from the tin, add the parsnips and leeks to the tin with the sherry vinegar and gently shake. Place the joint directly on top of the vegetables, and return to the oven for the remainder of the cooking time.

6. Remove the joint from the tin with the vegetables and transfer to a warmed platter. Cover and set aside to rest for 15–20 minutes.

7. Prepare the gravy: spoon off any excess fat from the roasting tin and discard. Place the tin over a medium heat and sprinkle over the flour. Stir well with a small whisk or spoon, add a little stock and stir again, scraping the base of the pan to release any rich, beefy sediment.

8. Add the remaining stock, wine and any meat juices from the platter, adjust the seasoning, if required, and simmer for 8–10 minutes, stirring occasionally until reduced to a well-flavoured gravy. Strain before serving.

9. Serve with potatoes, the caramelised vegetables and the gravy.

Rare – 20 min per 450g plus 20 min   **Medium** – 25 min per 450g plus 25 min   **Well done** – 30 min per 450g plus 30 min

Layered Parsnip and LANCASHIRE BAKE

Serves: 6 // Preparation time: 30 minutes // Cooking time: 45 minutes

INGREDIENTS

1 tbsp sunflower oil
1 large onion, sliced
1 garlic clove, crushed
750g parsnips, peeled
 and trimmed
2 tsp chopped fresh thyme
150g Lancashire
 cheese, crumbled
freshly grated nutmeg
salt and freshly ground
 black pepper
250ml hot vegetable stock

METHOD

1. Preheat the oven to 220°C/
   fan 200°C/425°F/gas mark 7.

2. Heat the oil in a frying pan, add the
   onions and sauté over a medium heat
   for 5 minutes or until golden. Season,
   then reduce the heat and cook over a
   low heat for a further 5 minutes until
   they are really tender and caramelised.

3. While the onions cook, diagonally
   slice the parsnips to a thickness
   of a one pound coin.

4. Lightly oil a 1.4 litre ovenproof dish.

5. Scatter half the onions over the base
   of the dish and top with half the
   parsnips, half the thyme, a third of
   the cheese, a little nutmeg and plenty
   of seasoning. Top with the remaining
   onions, parsnips and thyme, then
   pour over the stock. Sprinkle over the
   remaining cheese and season again.

6. Place the dish on a baking tray then
   cover with foil and bake for 30 minutes.
   Remove the foil then bake for a further
   20–25 minutes or until the parsnips
   are tender and the top nicely browned.
   Serve hot with roast meats or poultry.

WARM BEEF
and *Winter vegetable salad*
with HONEY AND MUSTARD DRESSING

Serves: 4 // Preparation time: 10 minutes

INGREDIENTS

2 large parsnips, peeled
  and cut into large dice
450g waxy potatoes, peeled
  and cut into large dice
2 small red onions, peeled
  and cut into quarters
salt and freshly ground
  black pepper
3 tbsp sunflower oil
100g fresh baby spinach leaves
450g lean sirloin, minute
  or flash-fry steaks

**For the honey and
mustard dressing**
4 tbsp olive oil
4 tsp red wine vinegar
4 tsp Dijon mustard
4 tsp runny honey

METHOD

1. Preheat the oven to 220C°/
   fan 200°C/425°F/gas mark 7.

2. Place the parsnips, potatoes and onions
   in a non-stick roasting tin, season
   and coat in 2 tablespoons of the oil.
   Roast in the oil for 35–40 minutes.
   Drain excess liquid if required and
   transfer to a large bowl. Cool slightly.

3. Meanwhile, make the dressing:
   place all the ingredients in a screw-
   topped jar and shake well.

4. Heat the remaining oil in a non-stick
   griddle or frying pan. Season the steaks
   and cook according to your preference.
   If you are using minute or flash-fry
   steaks, cook for 1–2 minutes on each
   side. Leave to rest on a warm plate for
   1–2 minutes then slice diagonally.

5. Whilst the vegetables are still
   warm, add the spinach leaves,
   beef and any meat juices from the
   plate. Pour over the dressing and
   toss gently. Serve immediately.

Based on a 2cm thick steak

Rare	Medium	Well done
2½ min on each side	4 min on each side	6 min on each side

Sausage and POTATO
CASSOULET

Serves: 4 // Preparation time: 10 minutes // Cooking time: 25–30 minutes

INGREDIENTS

1 tbsp olive oil
2 onions, sliced
1 carrot, peeled and chopped
2 garlic cloves, crushed
8 sausages
500g potatoes, cut
  into chunks
½ tsp chopped rosemary
1 tbsp Worcestershire sauce
250ml vegetable stock
1 can chopped tomatoes
1 can haricot beans, drained
1 tbsp chopped parsley

METHOD

1. Place a casserole pot over a medium heat, add half of the olive oil and cook the onions, garlic and carrot for 3–4 minutes until soft.

2. Meanwhile in a frying pan cook the sausages in the remaining oil until nicely browned.

3. Add the potatoes to the casserole pot with the rosemary, Worcestershire sauce and stock.

4. Add the sausages to the pot with the tinned tomatoes, haricot beans and parsley and cook with a lid on for 15–20 minutes, stirring every so often.

TOP TIP Look for the Red Tractor logo when shopping for your ingredients to ensure you are buying quality British produce.

Caramelised ONION and CHEDDAR SOUFFLÉ

Serves: 6 // Preparation time: 20 minutes // Cooking time: 15 minutes

INGREDIENTS

1 large onion, sliced
1 tbsp olive oil
50g sugar
40g butter
40g plain flour
225ml milk
4 eggs, separated
175g Cheddar cheese, grated
50g grainy mustard
salt and freshly ground
    black pepper

METHOD

1. Preheat the oven to
   180°C/fan 160°C/350°F/
   gas mark 4.

2. Lightly grease six 8 x 4cm
   deep ramekin dishes. Line
   the bottom of the dishes with
   a circle of greaseproof paper.

3. Gently heat the oil and
   cook the onions for 10
   minutes until translucent,
   add the sugar and turn the
   heat up to caramelise the
   onions. Keep to one side.

4. Melt the butter, stir in the
   flour to make a smooth
   paste and cook for 1 minute.
   Gradually stir in the milk,
   bring to the boil then reduce
   the heat to simmer and
   cook for a further minute.

5. Beat in one egg yolk at a
   time; add 100g of the cheese,
   mustard, salt and pepper.

6. Beat the egg whites in a
   clean bowl until stiff, stir
   into the cheese mixture.

7. Divide the onions between
   the ramekin dishes, then
   spoon the mixture on top
   of the onions. Bake for 20
   minutes. Leave to cool,
   then remove the soufflés
   by running a bladed knife
   around the edge of each dish.

8. Place the soufflés onto a
   baking sheet and sprinkle
   over the remaining cheese.
   Bake for 15 minutes
   until golden brown.

9. Serve with a rocket salad.

TOP TIP Look for the British Lion mark when buying your eggs to ensure you are buying quality British produce.

Rod Adlington

As we look forward to Christmas let's celebrate the farmers that rear the star of the festive table. Turkey producers across the country have honed their skills to bring you the tastiest of birds, and Rod Adlington is no exception.

Rod is a third generation poultry farmer running two farms near Kenilworth in Warwickshire. The main stay of his farming business are his free-range chickens, which he rears all year round, but every year Rod raises around 10,000 turkeys for Christmas. He favours using various types of rare breeds which are slow to develop and which he believes produce the best-tasting meat. Their flagship product is smoked turkey using oak and chestnut smoking chips. "Delicatessens can't get enough of it", Rod says. "They love its amazing taste. The fact that we produce something so different and unique compared with mainstream producers is what gets me up in the morning.

"I am hugely passionate about how and what we farm. And although we are busy all year, at Christmas time it comes manic. We always have an early start to the day and we check the birds' health and welfare to ensure all is as it should be. People want to know the bird they are buying has been reared well and will produce a great-tasting showpiece for their table.

"We also put the same emphasis on quality with our year-round chickens to ensure they produce succulent and quality meat. Our chicken portions are sold to many outlets from delicatessens to supermarkets, under the brand Label Anglais, which I am really pleased to say has been endorsed by chefs such as John Torode and accredited by Wholefoods.

"No two days are the same and I wear I variety of hats from completing office work and checking orders to ensuring the birds have everything they need. With farming I feel like I am control of my own destiny and I wouldn't have it any other way."

Given his passion for poultry it's not surprising to learn that Rod's favourite dish for supper is turkey breast, stuffed, rolled and wrapped in bacon.

Roast Turkey

with CUMBERLAND SAUSAGE, APPLE & HERB STUFFING

Serves: 8 // Preparation time: 30 minutes // Cooking time: 3 hours (approx.)

INGREDIENTS

2 tbsp oil

1 onion, peeled and chopped

6 small eating apples

175g fresh white breadcrumbs

2 tbsp freshly chopped thyme leaves

2 tbsp freshly chopped flat leaf parsley

450g Cumberland pork sausages, skins removed

1 egg, beaten

salt and freshly ground black pepper

5.4kg oven-ready turkey

50g butter, softened

a handful of fresh thyme sprigs

4 grilled rashers back bacon, to garnish

For the turkey gravy

juices from roasting

2 tbsp flour

700ml turkey or vegetable stock

a splash of red wine, Madeira or port

METHOD

1. Heat the oil in a frying pan and fry the chopped onion until just softened.

2. Peel, core and finely chop 3 of the apples and add to the pan. Cook for 2–3 minutes.

3. Leave to cool then mix with the breadcrumbs, herbs, sausages and egg. Season well with salt and freshly ground black pepper.

4. Preheat oven to 190°C/ fan 170°C/375°F/gas mark 5.

5. Fill the turkey neck with half the stuffing, then smooth down the flap of skin and tuck under the bird. Tie the turkey's legs together with string and fix the wings to each side of the bird with metal skewers. Calculate the cooking time by weighing the turkey – allow 18 minutes per 450g plus a further 18 minutes.

6. Shape the rest of the stuffing into 12 small balls, then put them in a roasting tin, cover and chill in the fridge.

7. Place the turkey in a roasting tin. Spread the butter over the skin, season and cover loosely with some buttered foil. Roast for the calculated time, basting occasionally with the juices from the roasting tin. Uncover for the last 45 minutes to allow the skin to brown (see timings above).

8. Transfer the turkey to a large warmed platter. Cover and leave in a warm place. Put 4 tablespoons of the cooking juices in a roasting tin. Cut the rest of the apples into wedges and toss into the juices. Roast in the oven with the tray of stuffing balls for 15–20 minutes until just golden.

9. To serve, put the stuffing balls, thyme sprigs and apple around the turkey, with the grilled bacon on top.

10. For the turkey gravy: pour nearly all the juice and fat from the roasting tin into a jug and skim off any excess fat from the top of the juices. Heat the roasting tin on the hob and stir in 2 tablespoons flour.

11. Cook, stirring with a wooden spoon, for 1 minute then gradually whisk in the turkey juices and about 700ml turkey or vegetable stock. Bring to the boil, stirring all the time, then allow to simmer until the gravy has thickened.

12. Add a large splash of red wine, Madeira or port and season with salt and pepper.

Creamed BRUSSELS SPROUTS with NUTMEG

Serves: 4 // Preparation time: 5 minutes // Cooking time: 10 minutes

INGREDIENTS

450g fresh Brussels sprouts,
   outer leaves and ends
   of stalks removed
30g butter
100ml double cream
1 tsp grated nutmeg
small bunch of fresh parsley,
   roughly chopped
black pepper

METHOD

1. In a pan of boiling water, simmer the
   sprouts for 8–10 minutes until just done.
   Drain, then tip into a food processor.

2. Add the butter, cream, nutmeg and three
   quarters of the parsley. Season to taste.

3. Blend until semi-smooth so
   it still has some texture.

4. Check the seasoning, then spoon
   into a warm serving dish and scatter
   with the remaining parsley and
   a good grind of black pepper.

TOP TIP You can add some diced crisp bacon to this recipe if you like. Also, any leftover Brussels sprouts can be used in a bubble and squeak – see p.82–83.

Honey-Glazed
PARSNIPS

Serves: 4 // Preparation and cooking time: 1 hour

INGREDIENTS

800g parsnips, peeled and cut
    into large bite-sized pieces
2 tbsp vegetable oil
2 tbsp butter
2 tbsp honey
1 tbsp lemon juice
2–3 tbsp fresh flat-leaf
    parsley, roughly chopped
1 tbsp chives, snipped
salt to taste

METHOD

1. Preheat the oven to 200°C/fan
   180°C/400°F/gas mark 6.

2. Place the parsnips on a baking tray
   and drizzle with the oil. Season
   with salt and toss well to coat.

3. Roast for around 35–40 minutes
   until soft to the tip of a knife, turning
   once. Remove from the oven.

4. To make the glaze, combine the
   butter, honey and lemon juice in
   a small saucepan and heat gently,
   stirring until melted and even.

5. Increase the oven temperature to
   240°C/fan 220°C/475°F/gas mark 9.

6. Brush the glaze onto the parsnips.
   Return to the oven until golden-brown,
   about 5–10 minutes; alternatively use
   the grill to finish off the parsnips.

7. Remove from the oven and serve
   garnished with the parsley and chives.

TOP TIP Look for the Red Tractor logo when shopping for your ingredients to ensure you are buying quality British produce.

Ollie Bartlett

Ollie Bartlett, of Alan Bartlett and Sons, specialises in growing carrots and parsnips, aiming to deliver the freshest product possible. For one of the world's biggest suppliers of these vegetables, Christmas might not seem such an exciting time!

Alan Bartlett and Sons is a fourth-generation, family-owned root vegetable company, whose sole focus is specialising in the growing, washing and packing of carrots and parsnips for UK supermarkets. They aim to look after the complete growing process from land preparation through to harvesting. It is a large farm currently renting in excess of 3,500 acres: the size of 2,650 football pitches. East Anglia is well known for growing these vegetables but the Bartletts also use land on the Moray Coast in Scotland for late season supply. They work with host farmers and form part of their rotation.

Like every farmer, Ollie keeps a close eye on his crops. "We work with agronomists to monitor and sample all of our crops each week to ensure they are healthy. Things like parsnip rust or carrot fly can cause havoc to our farming business and we sometimes change harvest plans to reduce any impact."

Their carrot varieties include Nairobi, Chantenay Red-Cored, and Nipomo bunched carrots; their parsnips include Javelin and Palace, all grown for their great flavour, resistance to pests and other problems, and robust growing quality.

"We never have two days the same on the farm," he adds. "We are always looking for what we can do better and more efficiently. Each day, harvesting starts at midnight so the crop can be delivered back to the factory ready for a 6am start. We wash, grade and pack throughout the day, ready for deliveries to our customers early the following morning. This means they could go from field to fork in as little as two days."

Unlike other vegetables, which are harvested and cold stored, carrots and parsnips are dug fresh every day, so the weather can sometimes be a challenge, especially as one of their main seasons is around Christmas, in the depths of winter. It is a particular peak for parsnips and volumes are enormous. They can supply up to three months' worth of parsnips in the 10 days leading up to Christmas Day alone.

Ollie jokes, "If you laid out all the carrots and parsnips we supply to UK supermarkets each year, they would stretch round the world twice!"

Because of his close connection with these vegetables, Ollie's favourite British dish has to be a Sunday roast, with beef and, of course, carrots and parsnips!

POTATO GRATIN

Serves: 4 // Preparation and cooking time: 2 hours 5 minutes

INGREDIENTS

1 litre whole milk

3 garlic cloves, crushed

3–4 rosemary sprigs, leaves only

2 bay leaves

1.5kg floury potatoes (such as King Edward or Maris Piper), peeled and thinly sliced

3 tbsp butter, softened

100g mature Cheddar cheese, grated

salt and freshly ground black pepper

METHOD

1. Preheat the oven to 170°C/ fan 150°C/325°F/gas mark 3.

2. Warm the milk, garlic, rosemary leaves, and bay leaves in a saucepan set over a medium heat until just simmering. Strain the milk into a jug; discard the garlic and herbs.

3. Rinse the potatoes in a bowl of water and then drain and pat dry with kitchen paper.

4. Grease a large baking dish with the butter and pour in some of the infused milk. Layer the potato slices into the dish in rows, seasoning generously with salt and pepper between each layer and again on top.

5. Pour over the rest of the milk and cover the dish with aluminium foil.

6. Bake for 1 hour 20–30 minutes until the potatoes are tender to the point of a knife.

7. Remove the foil and scatter the Cheddar cheese on top. Return the dish to the oven for about 15–20 minutes to brown the top.

8. Remove from the oven and let stand for 5 minutes before serving.

TOP TIP Look for the Red Tractor logo when shopping for your ingredients to ensure you are buying quality British produce.

PIGS IN Blankets

Serves: 8 // Preparation and cooking time: 10 minutes

INGREDIENTS

16 pork chipolatas
8 rashers streaky
   bacon, cut in half
freshly ground black pepper
bay leaves, to garnish

METHOD

1. Preheat the grill to hot.

2. Wrap the chipolatas with the bacon rashers, securing with toothpicks.

3. Arrange on a grill tray, spaced apart. Grill for 6–8 minutes, turning frequently, until the bacon is golden-brown and crisp.

4. Remove from the grill and let cool briefly before seasoning with some freshly ground black pepper and serving with a garnish of bay leaves.

TOP TIP
These pigs in blankets pair naturally with our bread stuffing recipe on p.48.

Bread STUFFING with ROSEMARY

Serves: 4 // Preparation and cooking time: 40 minutes

INGREDIENTS

250g day-old bread rolls,
   or white bread
300ml whole milk, warmed
1 tbsp butter
1 onion, finely chopped
50g bacon, chopped
1 rosemary sprig, leaves
   picked and finely chopped,
   plus extra sprigs to garnish
4 flat-leaf parsley sprigs, leaves
   picked and finely chopped
1 large egg, lightly beaten
100g Gruyère, finely diced
salt and freshly ground
   black pepper
fresh nutmeg, grated
2–3 tbsp clarified
   butter, for frying

METHOD

1. Cut the bread rolls into thin slices, place in a bowl, and pour over the warmed milk. Leave to soak for around 20 minutes.

2. Melt the butter in a frying pan set over a moderate heat. Add the onion, bacon and rosemary, and fry until the onion has softened, about 4–5 minutes.

3. Remove from the heat and stir in the parsley. Set aside to cool for 5 minutes.

4. After cooling, add to the soaked bread along with the egg and Gruyère. Season with plenty of salt, pepper, and nutmeg to taste.

5. Thoroughly mix together before shaping into rough balls between damp palms. Cover and chill for 5 minutes.

6. Heat the clarified butter in a large frying pan set over a moderate heat. Add the stuffing balls to the pan and fry on all sides until golden-brown, about 6–8 minutes.

7. Remove from the pan and stud with rosemary before serving.

CHRISTMAS SIDE DISHES
Gravy, BREAD SAUCE and CRANBERRY SAUCE

Serves: 8 // Preparation and cooking time: 1 hour 30 minutes

INGREDIENTS

For the cranberry sauce
juice and finely grated zest
    of 1 orange
400g fresh cranberries
175g caster sugar
125ml water

For the bread sauce
150g white bread, crusts
    removed and cut into
    5cm cubes
1 large onion, peeled
2 fresh bay leaves
8 whole cloves
750ml whole milk
3 tbsp butter
pinch of grated nutmeg
thyme sprigs, to garnish
salt and freshly ground
    black pepper

For the gravy
60g butter, cubed
35g plain flour
500ml beef stock

METHOD

1. **For the cranberry sauce:** combine orange juice, zest, cranberries, sugar, and water in a heavy-based saucepan. Cook over a medium heat, stirring from time to time, until the sugar has dissolved.

2. Cover with a lid and cook over a reduced heat until the mixture is thick and jammy, about 15–20 minutes; stir from time to time.

3. Spoon into a serving dish and leave to cool.

4. **For the bread sauce:** spread out the bread cubes on a large microwaveable plate or dish. Microwave on high for 4–5 minutes until dry to the touch and slightly crunchy. Carefully remove from the microwave and leave to cool.

5. Stud the bay leaves into the onion with the cloves.

6. Combine the studded onion and milk in a saucepan. Bring to a simmer before removing from the heat and letting stand for 15 minutes.

7. After 15 minutes, remove the onion and the bay leaf from the milk and set aside. Crumble the bread into the milk and leave to soak for 15 minutes.

8. Stir well and then cook over a low heat, stirring until thickened.

9. Once thickened, stir in the butter and some nutmeg, salt and pepper to taste.

10. **For the gravy:** melt the butter in a large saucepan set over a moderate heat.

11. Whisk in the flour until you have a smooth roux. Cook until dark blonde in colour.

12. Whisk in the beef stock in a slow, steady stream until fully incorporated. Bring to a simmer and then add the bay leaves and thyme sprigs.

13. Simmer over a medium heat, stirring from time to time, until thickened to your liking.

14. Serve warm alongside the bread sauce (garnished with thyme) and the cranberry sauce.

TRADITIONAL
Christmas PUDDING

Serves: 8 // Soaking time: 48 hours
// Preparation and cooking time: 8 hours 45 minutes

INGREDIENTS

150g currants
150g sultanas
150g dried prunes, chopped
175ml whisky
110g plain flour
115g fresh breadcrumbs
150g shredded suet
150g dark brown sugar
1 tsp ground cinnamon
¼ tsp ground cloves
1 tsp baking powder
3 large eggs
1 large cooking apple, cored,
   peeled and grated
zest of 1 large orange,
   finely grated
2 tbsp butter, softened

METHOD

1. Combine the dried fruit with the whisky in a large mixing bowl. Stir well and then cover and set aside to soak for at least two days, preferably longer, up to one week.

2. Combine the flour, breadcrumbs, suet, sugar, spices, baking powder, eggs, apple and orange zest in a large mixing bowl. Beat well until smooth, about 2–3 minutes.

3. Add the soaked fruits and their liquid and mix well to combine. Grease a 1.4kg pudding bowl with the softened butter.

4. Fill the bowl with the pudding mixture, pressing it down and compacting it firmly with the back of a wet tablespoon.

5. Place a lid or a saucer on top of the pudding bowl, making sure there is a little room between the lid and the pudding mixture. Tie the lid in place with kitchen string and then wrap the bowl with aluminium foil.

6. Place an upturned saucer in the base of a large saucepan. Place the pudding bowl on top of the saucer and then half-fill the saucepan with hot water. Bring to a simmer over a moderate heat, cover the saucepan with a lid, and steam the pudding over a slightly reduced heat for 5 hours, topping up the water as necessary when it starts to run a little low.

7. Carefully remove the pudding after 5 hours. Set aside to cool before storing in a dark, dry place for up to 6 months.

8. On the day you want to serve the pudding, rewrap the pudding bowl in fresh foil and steam again as before for 3 hours.

9. Carefully remove the pudding before turning out and serving with custard, cream, brandy butter or ice cream to taste.

Tom Wells

Farming on the edge of the fertile Lincolnshire Wolds, meet Tom Wells, a fourth generation farmer who mixes livestock and arable farming for perfect synergy.

Tom's farm lies in Barnetby Le Wold in North Lincolnshire, with a very mixed agenda. His cereal crops are produced for bread and beer, as well as animal feed. He grows our favourite brand of peas, as well as oilseed rape and all important sugar beet, all alongside sheep and cattle which benefit from his 'no-waste' attitude which sees crop residues and cover crops happily grazed away.

Tom enjoyed a gap year in New Zealand where he learnt to ride bulls but more importantly for his farm it's where he developed his passion for using livestock in the arable rotation scheme.

"It is hard work on such a mixed farm but I do get a kick out of it," Tom says. "There's no better feeling than getting up with the sun, spending your day with your animals and looking at flourishing crops, then putting your feet up with a well-earned beer. I love being outdoors and the synergies of using livestock in an arable rotation such as the sheep grazing off the sugar beet tops after the harvest. The waste is removed and muck put back into the soil to help its sustainability and ensuring it's ready for the next crop. It's what our ancestors did and I like combining the old knowledge of the land with modern day data and recording."

No day is typical for Tom. Every week he walks the land with an agronomist to look at crop health. You will often find him driving a pea viner with his hard working team working long days from mid-June through to mid-August. From the summer, they harvest cereal from midday once the dew has lifted, which means they can make the most of the sun to do the grain drying for them. Springtime sees lambing which brings nightly checks and early morning feeds. Tom says sugar beet is among the easier crops to grow providing you have the right soil type and seedbed. It involves autumn ploughing, light cultivation and precision drilling in spring, before lifting their 1,600 tonnes of grown sugar beets in late autumn for what is called the national sugar campaign, with crops intended for the Newark sugar factory.

Currently Tom is looking at the no-till approach to farming on some of his land, which means planting a crop with minimum disturbance of the soil. This is an idea which is beginning to take hold on many farms to avoid the many heavy machinery passes across the land, which compacts the soil, making it less attractive to soil's little helpers like worms.

With such a busy schedule, Tom still makes time to enjoy his favourite meal of Lincolnshire sausage, mash and onion gravy.

FESTIVE Chocolate LOG

Serves: 8 // Preparation and cooking time: 1 hour 5 minutes

INGREDIENTS

For the sponge
1 tbsp sunflower oil
4 medium eggs
120g caster sugar
2 tbsp warm water
125g plain flour, sifted
50g cocoa powder, sifted

For the filling
200ml whipping cream
2 tbsp icing sugar
1 tsp vanilla extract

For the ganache
150g dark chocolate, at least
  70% cocoa solids, chopped
200ml double cream
4 tbsp butter, cubed

To serve
icing sugar
holly leaves

METHOD

1. For the sponge: preheat the oven to 180°C/fan 160°C/350°F/gas mark 4. Line a 25 x 37cm Swiss roll tin with greaseproof paper. Grease the paper with sunflower oil.

2. Beat together the eggs and sugar in a large mixing bowl until thick, pale, and glossy, about 3–4 minutes.

3. Add the water, flour, and cocoa powder, folding gently to incorporate.

4. Spoon the batter into the prepared tin. Bake for 12–15 minutes until set and springy to the touch. Remove to a wire rack to cool.

5. Once cool, lift the sponge out of the tin using the greaseproof paper to help. Place on a flat work surface.

6. For the filling: whip the cream with the icing sugar and vanilla extract in a mixing bowl until softly peaked.

7. Spread the mixture over the sponge, stopping just short of the edges, before rolling tightly into a log. Cover and chill until needed.

8. For the ganache: place the chocolate into a heatproof bowl.

9. Warm the cream in a saucepan until it approaches boiling point. When it starts to boil, remove from the heat and pour over the chocolate. Leave to stand for 1 minute before adding the butter and stirring until you have a smooth, thick ganache. Let cool for 10 minutes.

10. Remove the roll from the fridge and place on a serving platter. Spread the cooled ganache all over the cake with a wet knife.

11. Lightly dust with icing sugar and decorate with holly leaves before serving.

TOP TIP Did you know Silver Spoon granulated, caster and icing sugar is the only sugar made from 100% British sugar beet? It takes about 4–6 beets to produce one pack of sugar.

BEETROOT AND APPLE Chutney

Serves: 8 // Preparation and cooking time: 1 hour 10 minutes

INGREDIENTS

500g cooked beetroot, diced
300g Bramley apples, peeled,
   cored and roughly chopped
100g raisins
1 onion, finely chopped
200ml malt vinegar
½ tsp ground ginger
pinch of grated nutmeg
¾ tsp salt
100g granulated sugar
1 tbsp cornflour

METHOD

1. Preheat the oven to 170°C/
   fan 150°C/325°F/gas mark
   3 and place a clean 450g
   jam jar in the oven with
   its lid to sterilise for 10
   minutes before removing.

2. In the meantime, combine
   the beetroot, apples,
   raisins, onion and vinegar
   in a large saucepan.

3. Set over a moderate heat
   and bring to the boil.
   Once boiling, reduce to a
   simmer and cook for about
   30 minutes until the apple
   is very soft and pulp-like.

4. Stir in the ground ginger,
   nutmeg, salt, sugar, and
   100ml water. Simmer for
   a further 15–20 minutes,
   stirring occasionally, until
   the chutney is easily broken
   down with a wooden spoon.

5. Remove from the heat and
   stir in the cornflour. Let
   cool briefly before spooning
   into the sterilised jar.

6. Cover with a wax paper
   circle before sealing with
   the sterilised lid. Store
   in a cool, dark place and
   refrigerate after opening.

TOP TIP
There are loads of brilliant British cheeses to choose from,
so why not try something different like Cornish Yarg or some
punchy Lincolnshire Poacher?

MINCE *Pies*
DUSTED *with* ICING SUGAR

Makes: 12 // Preparation and cooking time: 1 hour 10 minutes // Chill: 30 minutes

INGREDIENTS

For the pastry
350g plain flour
1 tbsp caster sugar
¼ tsp baking powder
pinch salt
180g unsalted butter,
    chilled and cubed
1 large egg
2–4 tbsp ice-cold water

For the filling
750g good quality
    mincemeat
3–4 tbsp whole milk

To serve
icing sugar

METHOD

1. For the pastry: combine the flour, sugar, baking powder, salt, and butter in a food processor. Pulse until the mixture resembles rough breadcrumbs.

2. Add the egg and 1–2 tablespoons of water, and pulse until a dough comes together around the blades; add more water if needed, pulsing to bring it together into a ball. Do not over-pulse.

3. Turn out the pastry, knead briefly, and then pat down and shape into a disc. Wrap with cling film and chill for 30 minutes.

4. For the filling: after chilling the pastry, preheat the oven to 180°C/fan 160°C/350°F/gas mark 4.

5. Roll out the pastry on a lightly floured surface to approximately 0.75cm thickness. Cut out 12 identical rounds large enough to line the base and sides of the holes of a cupcake tin; gather the remaining pastry into a ball and set aside.

6. Lift the pastry rounds into the holes of the tin and press well into the base and sides. Prick the bases with a fork and then use a wet tablespoon to fill with the mincemeat.

7. Re-roll the remaining ball of pastry to 0.5cm thickness and cut out 12 star shapes to serve as tops for the pies. Carefully arrange on top of the mincemeat filling.

8. Brush the tops of the pies with milk and bake for 25–35 minutes until the pastry is golden-brown and cooked through. Remove the tin to a wire rack to cool.

9. When ready to serve, turn out and dust with some icing sugar.

TOP
TIP
These mince pies are perfect served warm with a glass of mulled wine or brandy.

SWEET PASTRY HEARTS with *Jam filling*

Serves: 18 // Preparation and cooking time: 1 hour 10 minutes // Chill: 30 minutes

INGREDIENTS

For the jam
450g fresh raspberries
100ml tbsp water
400g granulated sugar
2 tsp butter

For the biscuits
375g plain flour, plus
extra for dusting
180g caster sugar
80g ground almonds
1 tsp lemon zest
275g butter, cubed
1 large egg
1 tsp vanilla extract

To serve
icing sugar

TOP TIP

Sterilise jars
Preheat the oven to 170°C/fan 150°C/325°F/gas mark 3 and place a clean 370ml jam jar in the oven with its lid to sterilise. Place a couple of saucers in the freezer; they will be needed for testing the jam's setting point.

METHOD

1. **For the jam:** Combine the raspberries and water in a large saucepan and cook over a medium heat, stirring occasionally, until the fruit softens. Once soft, add the sugar and stir well.

2. Reduce the heat and simmer the fruit and sugar for about 10 minutes until the sugar has dissolved, stirring the jam occasionally.

3. Remove from the heat and mash the raspberries. Pass the jam through a fine sieve into a bowl. Pour the jam mixture back into a clean saucepan and simmer for 5 minutes.

4. Spoon a little jam onto one of the frozen saucers, placing in the fridge for 1 minute. If it sets and crinkles a little when you drag your finger through it, it is ready. If not continue to boil the jam for another minute or so before testing again. When the jam is ready, remove from heat and stir in the butter. Pour into the sterilised jam jar and seal well with the lid. Cool at room temperature.

5. **For the biscuits:** Mix together the flour, sugar, ground almonds, and the lemon zest in a large mixing bowl. Create a well in the middle and place the butter in the well.

6. Crack the egg into the well and add the vanilla extract. Fold the ingredients together with a butter knife so that rough breadcrumbs are formed; you can also rub the ingredients together using your fingertips.

7. Quickly knead into a smooth dough and shape into a ball. Wrap in cling film and chill for 30 minutes.

8. After chilling, preheat the oven to 180°C/fan 160°C/350°F/gas mark 4 and line two large baking trays with greaseproof paper.

9. Roll out the dough on a lightly floured work surface to about 1 cm thickness. Cut out 36 heart-shaped pieces of dough using a heart-shaped cutter.

10. Arrange 18 on the lined trays. Use a smaller heart-shaped cutter to cut the middles out for the second layer, and arrange on a second tray.

11. Bake for about 12–15 minutes until pale golden and set. Remove the trays to wire racks to cool.

12. To serve: Once cool, spread the whole hearts with some jam. Top with the cut out hearts and dust with some icing sugar before serving.

Ross & Joe Davenport

Michael and Mary Davenport, their two sons Joe and Ross, and their herd of Friesian cows are producers of cheese in Lincolnshire.

The Davenport family are proud of their top herd management, looking after their 70-strong herd. Twelve years ago the big decision was made to use their top quality milk to enter the cheese market, in part to help combat poor returns on milk alone, and Cote Hill cheese was born.

It's a real family business, as Ross explains: "The farm had always produced very high quality milk but we needed to add more value so we decided to use some of it to make cheese. My father attended a cheese-making course, bought a 200 litre cheese vat and we produced our first batch of Cote Hill Blue in January 2005. I now look after the herd with him while my mother and Joe make the cheese."

The family are tenant farmers with 180 acres in an official Area of Outstanding Natural Beauty at the foot of the Lincolnshire Wolds. The cows graze the clover-rich pasture from April to October, with a buffer feed of maize, grass silage and some brewers' grains. These make the milk constituents less variable which means they are better for making cheese. This home-produced forage produces milk rich in butterfat and protein. The Davenports also use unpasteurised milk to allow the cheese to achieve individuality unique to Cote Hill Farm.

The cow parsley sprig logo also has a story behind it. Michael noticed the cows had grazed all of the cow parsley around the field edge in one day. It was obviously very palatable and in the morning when he lifted the bulk milk tank lid Michael noticed a lovely aroma of cow parsley. "There is so much connection between what the cows eat and how it influences the milk," he says.

Milking starts early in the morning, pumped directly from the parlour, into the cheese rooms next door. Three vats hold 1,000 litres in total. If cheese has been made the previous day, that batch is salted by hand, and the cheese moulds are washed and sterilised.

"We joke that 70% of cheese-making is washing up," says Ross. "Making cheese, especially from our milk, is such a rewarding and fascinating process. The fact that we see the cheeses stacked up at the end of the day, knowing that just a few hours ago it was just milk, still amazes me. No two days are the same as there is always some tinkering to the process to make great tasting cheese."

Cheese aside, given their milk supply, the family says one of their favourite dishes is cream, to go with strawberries in the summer.

Leek and Pear TART

Serves: 4 // Preparation time: 20 minutes // Cooking time: 25 minutes

INGREDIENTS

250g chilled puff pastry
2 medium size leeks,
    trimmed, washed and
    finely shredded
50g butter
½ tsp ground cinnamon
2 ripe pears, peeled,
    cored and sliced
75g goats' cheese
sprinkling of freshly
    grated nutmeg and
    ground cinnamon

METHOD

1. Preheat the oven to 220°C/
   fan 200°C/425°F/gas mark 7.

2. Roll out the pastry to the thickness
   of a pound coin and cut into a
   20cm round using a plate as a
   template. Rest on a baking sheet.

3. Gently sweat the shredded leaks
   in the butter for 2–3 minutes to
   soften but not brown. Season with
   cinnamon and pile on top of the pastry
   round leaving a 1cm clear rim.

4. Place the pear slices on top of the leeks.
   Dot with cubes of goats' cheese and
   sprinkle with nutmeg and pepper.

5. Bake in the oven until the pastry
   has risen and the cheese is
   bubbling. Serve whilst warm.

SPRING
An evocative promise of tantalising tastes brought
by the new green shoots of emerging spring

CREAMY Spring Onion SOUP

Serves: 4 // Preparation and cooking time: 45 minutes

INGREDIENTS

2 tbsp olive oil
1 bunch spring onions, sliced
1 onion, finely chopped
2 large floury potatoes,
    eg Desirée or Maris
    Piper, peeled and cubed
2 tbsp plain flour
750ml chicken stock
500ml whole milk
120ml double cream
1 small bunch chives, snipped
½ small bunch flat-leaf
    parsley, finely chopped
salt and freshly ground
    pepper to taste

METHOD

1. Heat the olive oil in a large saucepan set over a medium heat.

2. Add most of the spring onions (saving a small handful for the garnish), the onion, and a generous pinch of salt. Sweat for about 5 minutes until softened.

3. Stir in the potatoes and flour, and cook for 3 minutes stirring frequently.

4. Gradually whisk in the chicken stock in small additions until fully incorporated. Whisk in the milk and bring to the boil.

5. Reduce to a simmer for about 20 minutes or until the potato is very soft.

6. Purée with a hand blender or in batches in a blender.

7. Return the soup to a simmer before stirring in the cream. Season to taste with salt and pepper.

8. When ready to serve, ladle into warm bowls and top with the chives, parsley, and remaining spring onions as a garnish.

CREAM OF Broad Bean SOUP

Serves: 8 // Preparation time: 15 minutes // Cooking time: 20 minutes

INGREDIENTS

700g shelled broad beans
sprig of thyme
1 small onion
50g butter
35g flour
2 litres stock
8 tbsp double cream
chopped parsley or chervil
salt and freshly ground
   black pepper to taste

METHOD

1. Cook the beans in boiling water (just enough to cover) with the thyme. Drain and keep the liquid to make up the stock later. Refresh the beans under the cold tap and drain well again.

2. Meanwhile, peel and chop the onion finely. Fry in melted butter until soft.

3. Stir in the flour and cook for another 2–3 minutes.

4. Add the stock and bring to the boil. Season to taste and simmer for 10 minutes.

5. Keeping a few beans for garnish, add the rest to the soup. Simmer for a few minutes, then pass through a vegetable mill.

6. Just before serving, remove the outer skins from the kept beans and add to the soup.

7. Mix the cream and parsley or chervil together in a bowl.

8. Bring the soup back to the boil and pour a little onto the cream mixture. Stir well, tip back into the pan and reheat gently. Adjust seasoning and serve.

TOP TIP   Omit the cream and parsley or chervil for a lighter soup.

JERSEY POTATO SALAD with Radishes, Feta Cheese and MINT

Serves: 4 // Preparation and cooking time: 30 minutes

INGREDIENTS

For the salad
450g Jersey Royal
    potatoes, halved
1 red onion, sliced
125g feta style cheese,
    crumbled
5–6 radishes, sliced
1 tbsp oregano leaves,
    chopped
1 tbsp black peppercorns,
    crushed

For the dressing
4 tbsp olive oil
1 tbsp red wine vinegar
2 tbsp capers, drained
    and roughly chopped
1 garlic clove, finely chopped
salt to taste

To serve
mint leaves

METHOD

1. For the salad: cook the potatoes in a large saucepan of salted boiling water for 15–20 minutes until tender to the tip of a knife.

2. When ready, drain through a colander and rinse under cold, running water. Leave to cool.

3. Gently mix the potatoes with the remaining salad ingredients in a large serving bowl or platter.

4. For the dressing: whisk all the ingredients until well combined. Season to taste with some salt.

5. To serve: pour over the salad and toss thoroughly before serving with a garnish of mint leaves.

  TOP TIP Look for the Red Tractor logo when shopping for your ingredients to ensure you are buying quality British produce.

Spring ONION and FETA frittata

INGREDIENTS

200g new potatoes
6 spring onions, trimmed
1 thick slice carved ham,
    torn into pieces
1 tbsp oil
4 eggs, beaten
60g feta style cheese,
    crumbled
6 mint leaves, chopped

METHOD

1. Cube the potatoes into bite-sized chunks and parboil in water for 5–7 minutes.

2. Add the spring onions to the water for the last minute of cooking then drain.

3. Heat the oil in a medium-sized frying pan, add the potatoes, spring onions and ham pieces and toss in the oil.

4. Tip in the beaten eggs and stir a couple of times to coat and incorporate everything.

5. Sprinkle the feta and mint on top and allow to cook gently for 8–10 minutes until cooked halfway through. Meanwhile, heat the grill to hot.

6. Move the pan under the grill to cook from the top for 5–8 minutes until the frittata is golden and cooked through.

GREEN BEAN RISOTTO

Serves: 6 // Preparation time: 10 minutes // Cooking time: 35 minutes

INGREDIENTS

2 tbsp olive oil
150g fennel, chopped
225g risotto rice
1.2–1.3 litres vegetable stock
200ml dry white wine
salt and freshly ground
   black pepper to taste
115g French beans, halved
50g mangetout, halved
55g Parmesan cheese, grated,
   plus extra to serve

Herb butter
70g butter
1 tbsp chopped fennel fronds
2 tbsp chopped fresh chives
2 garlic cloves, finely chopped
¼ tsp roughly crushed
   black peppercorns

METHOD

1. First make the herb butter by beating all the ingredients together. Spoon onto a piece of greaseproof or non-stick baking parchment, shape into a roll and chill in the fridge while making the risotto.

2. Heat the oil in a large non-stick frying pan, add the fennel and fry for 5 minutes until softened and only just beginning to colour around the edges. Add the rice and stir.

3. Bring the stock to the boil in a saucepan. Stir the wine and a generous sprinkling of seasoning into the rice and then add a ladleful of hot stock. Simmer for about 20 minutes, stirring from time to time and topping up with ladlefuls of stock, as needed, until the rice is tender and nearly all the stock has been absorbed.

4. When the rice is almost cooked, about 5 minutes or so from the end of cooking, add the beans. When they are almost cooked, add the mangetout, cook for 2 minutes and then stir in the Parmesan and one-third of the herb butter, until melted.

5. Spoon into shallow soup bowls and top with slices of herb butter and extra Parmesan. Garnish with extra fennel fronds if liked.

TOP TIP

If you are not serving vegetarian diners, you might like to top the risotto with some crispy fried Parma ham or streaky bacon, cut into strips.

Diced beetroot, pumpkin or courgettes can also be added, or, if you are lucky enough to have some asparagus, then add some trimmed and halved spears along with the beans.

If you don't like fennel, replace it with leeks or onions and replace the fennel fronds with fresh sage.

Steven Pace

Nutrition for laying hens has always been very important to Doctor Steven Pace, a fourth generation poultry farmer from Cheshire, who gained a PhD to further his knowledge on the subject.

Steven runs his farm with both parents and grandparents. It is a mixed operation, including arable land, sheep and, most importantly, laying hens.

Steven's main responsibilities are managing the free-range chickens and a feed mill. The business has expanded from 1,000 birds in 1930 to around 60,000 free range birds today. They try to do as much as possible themselves to drive down costs and to keep the farm as sustainable as possible. To this end, they use their own crops and mill as feed, rear the hens from day-old chicks, before finally packing and grading the eggs all on the farm. "By doing this we can produce a great quality product," Steven remarks. "It works well as a system because the sheep keep the grass tidy in the ranges, the crops feed the hens and the hen manure goes back onto our land to fertilise the crops. Most of our eggs are sold to local retailers and restaurants but some of them do go to a larger egg packer, who supplies the national supermarkets."

Steven thinks the best thing about his job is its variety. "I never know what each day will hold, but looking after the birds' health is a priority. A typical day starts with general poultry husbandry, checking the birds, feeding and watering the flock. By the time I finish, the egg grading staff have started to come in and I will help with that too. We have a great team who will check every egg, removing any that don't reach the grade. After helping to set up the grader, I normally head to the feed mill to check it is busy doing its job. I have to make about 10 tonnes of feed every day to feed our hens, so it's important it starts up as soon as possible. It takes the feed mill about 15 minutes to make one tonne of feed. We mix a variety of ingredients, including wheat, barley and oats all grown on our farm."

After these routine tasks, Steven also spends time in the office selling his eggs, as well as driving a tractor around the fields, fixing fences around the ranges or working with the sheep.

It is hardly surprising that at the end of a long day, Steven likes to dine on gammon, egg and chips, getting the eggs fresh from the farm.

Bubble and SQUEAK

Serves: 4 // Preparation and cooking time: 20 minutes

INGREDIENTS

3 tbsp unsalted butter
1 onion, finely chopped
pinch of salt
500g roast potatoes,
   roughly chopped
300g steamed cabbage,
   chopped
salt and freshly ground
   black pepper to taste

METHOD

1. Melt 1 tablespoon of the butter in
   a large non-stick frying or sauté
   pan set over a medium heat.

2. Add the onion and a pinch of salt, sweating
   until softened, about 5 minutes.

3. Stir in the remaining butter and let it melt
   before adding the chopped roast potatoes,
   cabbage, and plenty of salt and pepper.

4. Fry for 6–8 minutes, stirring and tossing
   from time to time, until the potatoes
   are golden and crisp at their edges.

5. Adjust seasoning to taste before
   serving straight from the pan.

  TOP TIP Look for the Red Tractor logo when shopping for your ingredients to ensure you are buying quality British produce.

Garlic and Lemon
ROAST CHICKEN

Serves: 4 // Preparation time: 10 minutes // Cooking time: 1 hour

INGREDIENTS

1 medium chicken
spray cooking oil
1 garlic bulb
salt and freshly ground
   black pepper
2 lemons
½ pint chicken stock

METHOD

1. Preheat the oven to 200°C/ fan 180°C/400°F/gas mark 6.

2. Place the chicken in a roasting tray and spray with cooking oil.

3. Rub a little salt and pepper over the skin evenly.

4. Cut both the lemons and squeeze the juice over the skin of the chicken; don't throw away the lemon shells.

5. Break off the garlic cloves from the bulb but don't remove the skin. Place one clove in each of the lemon shells and stuff them inside the chicken.

6. Scatter the rest of the garlic cloves around the chicken in the roasting tray. Roast for about 1 hour until cooked, frequently spooning the juices over the bird. Make sure the chicken is thoroughly cooked by checking to see if the juices run clear.

7. When cooked, take the chicken out of the oven and put on to a carving board, holding it over the roasting tray for a few seconds to get rid of any excess juice. Cover with foil and leave while you make the gravy.

8. Drain off any excess oil in the roasting tin then place the tin on the hob. Squash the cooked garlic cloves with a fork and remove the skins. When the tin is heated add the stock – use a wooden spoon to scrape off any pieces and stir into the gravy.

9. Bring it to the boil quickly then turn the heat down and reduce the liquid a little. Strain gravy into a jug, divide up the meat and serve with the gravy.

Pork Belly on A Bed of Mashed Potatoes

Serves: 4 // Preparation and cooking time: 3 hours

INGREDIENTS

For the pork
1 pork belly roast,
   about 1.5kg,
   with skin
2 tbsp honey
3 tbsp sunflower oil
salt and freshly
   ground black
   pepper to taste

**For the mashed
potato**
1.2kg floury potatoes
   (eg Maris Piper,
   preferably) peeled
   and cut into chunks
120g unsalted
   butter, cubed
1 small leek, halved,
   sliced, washed,
   and drained
100ml double cream

For the gravy
120ml Madeira
   wine or sherry
100ml chicken stock

METHOD

1. For the pork: preheat the oven to 140°C/fan 120°C/275°F/gas mark 1. Line a roasting tray with a trivet large enough to hold the pork belly.

2. Wash the pork belly and thoroughly dry with kitchen paper. Score the skin side at 1.25cm intervals using the tip of a sharp knife. Flip the belly over and puncture the meat all over with the tip of the knife.

3. Stir together the honey and 2 tablespoons of the oil in a bowl. Rub the mixture onto the meat side of the belly.

4. Sit the belly, skin-side facing up, on the trivet in the tray. Rub the skin with the remaining oil and season generously with salt and pepper. Roast for about 2 hours and 5–15 minutes until the meat is tender and the skin looks dry.

5. For the potatoes: cook the potatoes in a large saucepan of salted, boiling water until tender to the tip of a knife, about 15–20 minutes.

6. In the meantime, melt a few knobs of butter in a large sauté pan set over a medium heat.

7. Add the leek and a generous pinch of salt, sweating until softened and turning translucent, about 8–10 minutes. Set aside to cool.

8. Drain the potatoes when ready. Tip back into the saucepan they were cooked in and add the remaining butter. Mash thoroughly until smooth. Add the cream and the sweated leeks, mash again, and season to taste with salt and pepper.

9. When the pork is ready, remove it from the oven and transfer to a grilling tray. Turn the grill on. Brush the skin side with a thin layer of the pan juices and then glaze under the hot grill until the skin is golden and crisp. Remove from the tray and leave to rest, covered loosely with foil, for at least 10 minutes.

10. For the gravy: place the roasting tray used for the pork over a medium heat. Add the Madeira or sherry and let it bubble to reduce by at least two-thirds.

11. Stir in the stock and bring to the boil. Reduce slightly until thickened. Adjust seasoning to taste with salt and pepper as needed.

12. Serve pieces of the pork on a pile of mash and dress with the gravy.

FILLET OF BEEF
with Tomatoes and POTATOES

Serves: 4 // Preparation and cooking time: 1 hour

INGREDIENTS

300g Jersey Royal
    potatoes, scrubbed
400g beef fillet, trimmed
    of excess fat
2 tbsp sunflower oil
salt and freshly ground
    black pepper to taste
125ml dry red wine
225g mixed wild mushrooms,
    brushed clean and
    roughly chopped
6 vine tomatoes, cored
    and quartered
6 spring onions, trimmed
2–3 rosemary sprigs
3–4 thyme sprigs
2–3 tbsp olive oil

METHOD

1. Cook the potatoes in a
   large saucepan of salted,
   boiling water until tender
   to the tip of a knife,
   about 15–20 minutes.

2. In the meantime, rub
   the steak with sunflower
   oil. Season generously
   with salt and pepper.

3. Heat a cast-iron or heavy-
   based frying pan over a
   high heat until it just starts
   to smoke. Carefully place
   the steak in the pan and
   quickly sear until golden-
   brown all over. Remove
   to a roasting dish.

4. Deglaze the pan with
   the red wine, letting it
   reduce by half. Set aside.

5. Preheat the oven to
   220°C/fan 200°C/425°F/
   gas mark 7.

6. Drain the potatoes when
   ready. Toss with the
   mushrooms, tomatoes, spring
   onions, herbs, olive oil, and
   some salt and pepper to taste.

7. Arrange in the roasting
   dish, positioning the steak
   on top. Pour over the
   deglazed pan juices.

8. Roast for 10 minutes until
   the steak is firm to the
   touch with a slight spring.

9. Remove from the oven and
   remove the steak from the
   dish. Cover loosely with
   aluminium foil and let rest.

10. Return the vegetables to
    the oven and roast for a
    further 10–15 minutes until
    coloured. Remove from
    the oven when ready.

11. Slice the steak into thin
    slices. Arrange the vegetables
    and juices from the dish
    onto plates. Add the steak
    slices on top and serve.

CHICKEN and Roast Vegetable PASTA

Serves: 4 // Preparation time: 5 minutes // Cooking time: 15 minutes

INGREDIENTS

1 red, yellow or green
   pepper, seeded and cubed
1 courgette, cut into chunks
1 red onion, quartered
2 firm tomatoes, halved
2 tbsp oil
4 skinless chicken fillets,
   cut into chunks
salt and freshly ground
   black pepper
pasta shapes (cook
   as per packet)
freshly chopped herbs
   to garnish

METHOD

1. Put the vegetables into a roasting pan and drizzle with most of the oil. Season with salt and pepper and place under a hot grill for 5–10 minutes, turning occasionally, until softened and slightly charred.

2. Wipe a large frying pan with the remaining oil, heat the pan and add the chicken pieces. Cook over a high heat for about 4–5 minutes, turning the chicken frequently until it is a golden brown all over.

3. Meanwhile, cook the pasta as per pack instructions in a large pan of boiling water. Drain and return to the pan.

4. Add the charred vegetables and chicken to the pasta and toss. Serve with a herb garnish.

TOP TIP   Look for the Red Tractor logo when shopping for your ingredients to ensure you are buying quality British produce.

STEAK and Chermoula SALAD

Serves: 4 // Marinating time: 30 minutes // Cooking time: 40 minutes

INGREDIENTS

For the chermoula
2 garlic cloves
2 tbsp white vinegar
juice of 1 lemon
2 tsp ground paprika
2 tsp ground cumin
1 red chilli, seeded
2 tbsp olive oil
salt to taste

For the salad
4 lamb rump steaks
500g baby new potatoes,
    scrubbed and thickly sliced
225g mixed dwarf beans,
    thickly sliced, and runner
    beans, thinly shredded
1 small red onion,
    thinly sliced
edible flower petals,
    sprouting radish seeds or
    fresh parsley, to garnish

METHOD

1. Prepare the chermoula using the top tip below. Put the steaks in a single layer in a non-metallic dish and pour over a generous third of the dressing, reserving the remainder. Leave to marinate for 30 minutes.

2. Add the potatoes to a saucepan of boiling water and cook for 15 minutes.

3. Add all the beans to the pan and cook for another 4–5 minutes until just tender.

4. Meanwhile, preheat a non-stick frying pan. Lift the steaks out of the marinade, reserving the marinade, add the steaks to the pan and fry for 10 minutes, turning once, until browned on the outside and with just a hint of pink in the centre. Set aside.

5. Drain the vegetables and place in a large shallow dish. Stir the reserved dressing together once more, add to the vegetables with the onion and toss together.

6. Add the reserved marinade to the frying pan, cook for 1 minute and then pour over the salad. Adjust the seasoning if needed.

7. Thinly slice the steaks and arrange on top of the salad. Garnish with edible flower petals, sprouting radish seeds or chopped parsley. Serve while hot.

TOP TIP Chermoula is a classic Moroccan marinade that can be used with vegetables, meat or fish. To make this tasty paste simply mix the ingredients above in a bowl and blend using a food processor until you have a smooth consistency.

Beef WELLINGTON

Serves: 6 // Preparation time: 20 minutes
// Cooking time: 1 hour–1 hour 15 minutes

INGREDIENTS

2 tbsp oil
675g fillet of beef (thick end)
2 medium onions, peeled
   and finely chopped
100g chestnut mushrooms,
   chopped
2 level tbsp chopped
   fresh parsley
1 level tsp chopped
   fresh thyme
1–2 cloves garlic, crushed
3–4 tbsp freshly made
   breadcrumbs
salt and pepper to taste
500g block of puff
   pastry, defrosted
beaten egg to glaze

METHOD

1. Heat the oil in a pan and fry the fillet of beef on all sides until well sealed and lightly browned – about 8 minutes. Remove from the heat and leave to cool.

2. Fry the onions in the same fat until soft and lightly coloured, add the mushrooms and continue cooking for a few minutes more. Remove from the heat and mix in the herbs, garlic, breadcrumbs and plenty of seasoning. Allow to cool.

3. Preheat the oven to 220°C/ fan 200°C/425°F/gas mark 7.

4. Roll out the pastry to a rectangle large enough to enclose the beef.

5. Spread the mushroom mixture over the pastry leaving edges around for sealing, and place the beef on top. Wrap the beef completely in the pastry, damping the edges to seal, then place on a greased baking sheet with the seam underneath and the ends tucked under.

6. Decorate the top with a double row of leaves made from the pastry trimmings. Glaze well and make one or two small slits.

7. Bake for about 40 minutes until the pastry is well puffed and browned. At this stage the beef should be rare. If more cooking is required lower the temperature to moderate (180°C/fan 160°C/350°F/gas mark 4) and cook for a further 15 minutes for medium to well done. Serve hot or cold.

TOP TIP Look for the Red Tractor logo when shopping for your ingredients to ensure you are buying quality British produce.

Janet Oldroyd

Janet Oldroyd is referred to as the High Priestess of Rhubarb, which she acknowledges as an honour. An award-winning grower with no plans for retirement, she still enjoys growing and listening to her jewel-in-the-crown crop.

It was Janet's father, Ken, who took the brave step of dramatically expanding Oldroyd's rhubarb production, at a time when many were leaving the industry. Although it was her great-grandfather who first took the Oldroyds into forcing rhubarb, after he was taught the closely guarded secrets of forcing it by a friend. It became a real family concern, with husbands, in-laws and sons all taking the business forward over time. By the 1960s, forced rhubarb had become a dying industry, leading to Ken forming the Yorkshire Rhubarb Growers Ltd. With the cooperative support behind them, growers also relied on research into new varieties – Stockbridge Arrow, Stockbridge Harbinger and Cawood Delight – with more research made into yield and quality to offset increasing costs and falling prices. Ken was awarded the highly-prized Harlow Carr Medal in 1975 for his services to the industry. Of the 800 acres they farm now, 200 are down to rhubarb. Outdoors, the family produces almost 800 tonnes yearly, and indoors 200 tonnes of Yorkshire forced rhubarb.

Janet joined her family's company in 1979 following a career as a medical scientific officer; her sons now make up the fifth generation in this family business. Things have changed over the years, each generation having their own difficulties to overcome. Today, climate change has posed real problems, with changes in weather resulting in growers losing two months from the forced growing season. Other difficulties include the loss of rented land for growing. Although Janet's family have the luxury of owning some land because of her father's enterprising attitude, suitable land for rent or purchase in the area is now in short supply for their rhubarb and strawberry crops. And don't mention Himalayan balsam – it has become a real nuisance weed in rhubarb crops. Janet's son Lindsay is involved in research against this pesky invader.

Janet has been given many acknowledgements, not only for growing but also for promoting rhubarb as part of the tourist attractions of the area. "I take a real delight in promoting the crop through our rhubarb tours, which are really popular with tourists due to the links with forced rhubarb within this area of Yorkshire," said Janet. "It always inspires me when people see the crop for the first time growing in our dark houses and are amazed to hear the crop growing. My mission is to educate the public as to the benefits this plant has to offer. Rhubarb is in our family's blood, and hopefully I will be around to advise or inspire many more generations of Oldroyds to come."

The family continue to grow, harvest and propagate this very special crop. They still all enjoy a rhubarb and custard pudding.

RHUBARB and Ginger FOOL

Serves: 4 // Preparation time: 5 minutes // Cooking time: 10–15 minutes

INGREDIENTS

450g rhubarb,
   trimmed and diced
75g golden caster sugar
150ml whipping cream
3 tbsp stem ginger syrup
300ml Greek yoghurt
2 pieces stem ginger,
   finely chopped
sweet biscuits, to serve

METHOD

1. Place the rhubarb in a frying pan with the sugar and 4 tablespoons of water.

2. Heat gently until the sugar dissolves, then simmer for 10–15 minutes until the rhubarb is very soft. Leave to cool.

3. In a large bowl, whip the cream and stem ginger syrup until softly peaking. Fold in the yoghurt and nearly all the rhubarb and stem ginger pieces.

4. Divide the fool between four serving dishes. Top with the rest of the rhubarb and ginger and serve with sweet biscuits.

RHUBARB
Muffins

Makes: 12 // Preparation and cooking time: 45 minutes

INGREDIENTS

110g golden caster sugar
65g butter, softened
250g sour cream
2 large eggs, beaten
200g plain flour, sifted
¾ tsp bicarbonate of soda
¼ tsp salt
¼ tsp ground cinnamon
¼ tsp ground nutmeg
225g forced rhubarb
  (or regular rhubarb
  if not available),
  trimmed and diced
1 tbsp icing sugar, to serve

METHOD

1. Preheat the oven to 190°C/fan 170°C/375°F/gas mark 5. Line a 12-hole muffin or cupcake tin with paper muffin cases.

2. Cream together the sugar and butter in a large mixing bowl with an electric mixer until fluffy, about 3 minutes.

3. Beat in the eggs, one by one, followed by the sour cream.

4. Add the flour, bicarbonate of soda, salt, and ground spices to the bowl. Stir well until you have a rough batter; it shouldn't be totally smooth.

5. Divide the batter between the muffin cases and top each with rhubarb, pressing the pieces into the batter.

6. Bake for about 25–30 minutes until risen and springy to the touch when pressed; a toothpick should come out clean from their centres. Remove to a wire rack to cool.

7. When ready to serve, very lightly dust with icing sugar.

Rhubarb CRUMBLE CAKE

Serves: 8 // Preparation and cooking time: 1 hour 30 minutes

INGREDIENTS

For the cake
600g forced rhubarb,
   or regular rhubarb if
   forced not available,
   trimmed and chopped
120g caster sugar
100ml water
250g unsalted butter,
   softened
250g golden caster sugar
5 large eggs
2 tsp vanilla extract
300g plain flour, sifted
2 tsp baking powder
½ tsp ground allspice

For the crumble topping
180g plain flour
50g ground almonds
120g golden caster sugar
pinch of salt
120g unsalted butter,
   cold and cubed
icing sugar, to serve

METHOD

1. For the cake: preheat the oven to 180°C/ fan 160°C/350°F/gas mark 4. Grease and line the base and sides of a rectangular baking dish with some greaseproof paper.

2. Combine the rhubarb, caster sugar and water in a heavy-based saucepan. Cover and cook over a medium heat until the sugar has dissolved.

3. Remove the cover and continue to cook for about 6–8 minutes until the rhubarb is very soft to the tip of a knife. Remove from the heat and strain the rhubarb through a colander, collecting the juice in a bowl underneath.

4. Cream together the butter and golden caster sugar in a large mixing bowl with an electric mixer, about 3–4 minutes.

5. Thoroughly beat in the eggs, one by one, followed by the vanilla extract.

6. Add the flour, baking powder, and ground allspice, folding into the mixture until you have a smooth batter.

7. Spoon the batter into the prepared dish. Top with the strained rhubarb in an even layer.

8. For the crumble topping: rub together the flour, ground almonds, sugar, salt, and butter in a mixing bowl until rough clumps form.

9. Scatter over the rhubarb. Bake the cake for about 45–50 minutes until the cake is golden-brown and risen at the edges; a toothpick or cake tester should come out clean from the base in the middle of the cake. Remove to a wire rack to cool.

10. To serve: when ready to serve, lift out the cake from the dish using the greaseproof paper to help. Discard the paper. Lightly dust the cake with icing sugar before slicing and serving.

Tom Martin

Meet Tom Martin, a sixth generation farmer, growing cereals for us and the birds on his farm in North Cambridgeshire. The family has been farming on this heavy clay ridge for many years.

Tom used to work in the film industry, where he spent ten years based in London. He returned to the family farm based on the fairly flat land of Cambridgeshire in May 2015, a proud and passionate farmer, not only about local, seasonal, British food, but also about showing consumers (everyone!) what happens on the other side of the farm gate.

The farm practises minimum tillage, growing wheat and barley, as well as rapeseed and linseed. In the past few years, they have also experimented with canary grass (grown for birdseed), mustard, and sunflowers – these last two are grown to be mixed in with their own linseed and a neighbour's spring peas to produce a home-grown cover crop mix. This helps to improve soil structure and fixes nitrogen from the atmosphere. And they also fatten sheep and run a direct-to-consumer boxed lamb scheme at www.villagefarm.org.uk.

Tom works with his dad and business partner, George, and says every day brings a new challenge. They could be chasing sheep one minute, and loading wheat the next, or meeting with any of the groups Tom is involved in.

"I farm because I love it," says Tom. "And I keep farming because it's exciting, the challenges are huge, because every day is different, and because no one knows what's coming around the corner. I love being outside and I would definitely describe myself as a conservation farmer. I believe the natural world around us is one of our greatest gifts and stewarding the land is the highest calling. One of my favourite areas on the farm is our 'overwintering bird', and 'butterfly and bee' areas planted with crop mixes. One of my proudest achievements is seeing the wildlife that is thriving on the farm.

"I think farming is, or should be, one big, united family, as we all have a joint goal of feeding our growing and diverse population. I have travelled to Singapore to take part in the Royal Agricultural Societies of the Commonwealth conference touring Singapore and Malaysia with HRH The Princess Royal, and I am planning trips to Germany and to Austria to visit farms there. I believe we all have a lot to learn from one another.

"I take an active interest in politics, and have hosted MPs and MEPs on the farm to talk to them about the important issues facing farming, as well as numerous other groups and interested parties. I also love being involved in championing farming both within the industry and, more typically, beyond."

With his own cereal crops in mind, Tom's favourite British dish is blackberry and apple crumble using his wife Lisa's great recipe for the topping.

Hot Cross BUNS

Makes: 12 // Preparation and cooking time: 1 hour 30 minutes

INGREDIENTS

For the buns
500g plain flour
3 tsp active dried yeast
2 tsp mixed spice
½ tsp ground cinnamon
60g golden caster sugar
1 tsp salt
1 small unwaxed lemon,
    zest only, finely grated
450ml tepid water, plus
    extra as needed
120g unsalted butter, softened
200g raisins
1 tbsp mixed candied
    peel, chopped

For the crosses
125g plain flour
3 tsp cornflour
3 tbsp golden caster sugar
water to mix

For the glaze
175g apricot jam, or
    marmalade, warmed

METHOD

1. For the buns: line a large square baking tray with greaseproof paper.

2. Combine the flour, yeast, spices, sugar, salt, and lemon zest in a mixing bowl and stir well to mix.

3. Add 400ml of the water, and the butter, and mix until the water is incorporated. Beat until well blended and the consistency of a thick cake batter, adding more water if the mixture is too thick.

4. Stir in the raisins and candied peel. Place the bowl in a warm place and leave for about 25–30 minutes until the mixture is slightly swollen.

5. For the crosses: combine the flour, cornflour and sugar into a small bowl and gradually whisk in enough water to make a smooth pipeable paste. Spoon into a piping bag fitted with a thin, round nozzle.

6. Make 12 mounds of the dough mixture and place on the baking tray in four rows of three, side by side. Pipe crosses on top of each bun with the prepared paste. Leave to rise in a warm place for 1 hour.

7. Preheat the oven to 180°C/ fan 160°C/350°F/gas mark 4. After the dough has risen, bake for about 30–40 minutes until golden, risen, and dry to the touch.

8. To glaze: remove the buns from the oven and brush all over with the warmed jam before serving.

SIMNEL *Cake*

Serves: 8 // Preparation and cooking time: 2 hours 30 minutes

INGREDIENTS

For the cake
150g butter, softened
125g soft light brown sugar
3 large eggs, beaten
2 tbsp whole milk
175g plain flour
1 tsp baking powder
¼ tsp salt
1 tsp ground mixed spice
½ tsp grated nutmeg
½ tsp ground cinnamon
100g raisins
100g currants
175g sultanas
40g chopped candied peel
500g yellow marzipan
icing sugar, for dusting

To decorate
icing sugar
2–3 tbsp apricot jam,
    warmed for glazing
1 small egg, beaten
chocolate mini eggs

METHOD

1. For the cake: preheat the oven to 170°C/fan 150°C/325°F/gas mark 3. Grease and line the base of an 18cm springform cake tin with greaseproof paper.

2. Cream together the butter and sugar in a large mixing bowl with an electric mixer until fluffy for about 3 minutes.

3. Gradually beat in the eggs, a little at a time, until fully incorporated. Beat in the milk.

4. Sift the flour, baking powder, salt, and spices together in a separate bowl and add to the mixture, alternately, with the dried fruits and candied peel. Mix well. Spoon half the batter into the tin and smooth the top.

5. Roll out most of the marzipan (reserve enough for the decoration) on a surface lightly dusted with icing sugar and trim into two rounds, large enough to fit the cake tin.

6. Place one round on top of the cake mixture and press lightly. Cover with the rest of the cake batter and smooth the top, hollowing the centre slightly.

7. Bake for about one and a half hours until cooked through; a cake tester will come out clean from the centre. Remove from the oven and allow to cool completely in the tin.

8. Increase the oven temperature to 200°C/ fan 180°C/400°F/ gas mark 6.

9. To decorate: brush the top of the cake with warmed apricot jam. Lay the remaining circle of marzipan on top of the cake. Form 11 small balls from the reserved marzipan and place them around the edge in a circle.

10. Form the marzipan trimmings into a plait and place in the centre of the marzipan top. Brush the marzipan with beaten egg and return the cake to the oven until the marzipan is glazed and lightly brown.

11. Remove from the oven and allow to cool in the tin for 20 minutes. Transfer to a wire rack to cool completely.

SUMMER

As things hot up it is time to celebrate an abundance
of British fare from our home-grown summer larder

Asparagus and LENTILS with POACHED EGGS

Serves: 2 // Preparation time: 10 minutes // Cooking time: 25 minutes

INGREDIENTS

1 bundle British asparagus
   (approx. 250g)
3 tbsp olive oil
salt and freshly ground
   black pepper
1 small red onion, finely diced
2 sticks celery, finely chopped
1 clove garlic, crushed
1 small red chilli, deseeded
   and finely chopped
400g can brown lentils,
   drained
150g baby cherry tomatoes,
   sliced in half
3 tbsp chopped fresh
   coriander
2 large free range eggs

METHOD

1. Preheat oven to 200°C/fan 180°C
   400°F/gas mark 6.

2. Trim the woody ends from the asparagus and
   brush the spears with 1 tablespoon of oil. Place the
   asparagus in a shallow ovenproof dish or roasting
   tin, season with a little salt and freshly-ground black
   pepper and cook for 6–8 minutes or until tender.

3. Heat the remaining oil in a non-stick frying pan, add
   the onion, celery, garlic and chilli and sauté over a
   low heat for 5–10 minutes or until the onions are soft.

4. Add the lentils and tomatoes and cook for a further
   5 minutes or until the lentils are hot. Remove from
   the heat and stir in the coriander.

5. To poach the eggs, place a large saucepan of water
   on the hob and bring to a fast rolling boil. Crack the
   eggs into the boiling water and immediately lower
   the heat to low–medium for 2 minutes.

6. Divide the lentil mixture between two serving bowls,
   lay the asparagus over the lentil mixture. Using a
   slotted spoon, remove the eggs from the water and
   gently place on the asparagus. Break the eggs open
   slightly to allow the yolks to run out. Sprinkle over
   the coriander and serve immediately.

PEPPER and TOMATO Soup

Serves: 4 // Preparation time: 5 minutes // Cooking time: 15 minutes

INGREDIENTS

1 tbsp mild olive oil
1 onion, diced
2 bell peppers, diced
500ml tomato passata
500ml vegetable stock
1 tbsp sundried tomato paste
5 basil leaves
salt and pepper to taste
20g crumbled goats' cheese

METHOD

1. Warm the oil and fry the onion until transparent.

2. Add the peppers to the onion and cook for about 5–10 minutes until the peppers are soft.

3. Add the remaining ingredients and simmer for about 5 minutes.

4. Blend the soup using a stick blender until smooth.

5. Taste and add more basil, salt and pepper as required.

6. Serve with a few pieces of the goats' cheese crumbed over the top.

  TOP TIP Look for the Red Tractor logo when shopping for your ingredients to ensure you are buying quality British produce.

MEET ~the~ FARMER

Chris Moore

Chris Moore, a fourth generation farmer, farms his beetroot on
the Isle of Axholme, near Epworth, with his brother David.

The William F. Moore farm takes its name from Chris' grandfather. Now Chris is hoping his son George may well be the fifth generation to take over the mixed agricultural farm, with beetroot forming a large part of the produce. They are in the process of joining LEAF (Linking Environment And Farming), so this is an important aspect of the brothers' ambitions. Provenance of their product is something of which they are also incredibly proud, and Chris was one of the founding farmers who helped to launch the Red Tractor Scheme some years ago. The logo helps shoppers to trace the food they are buying back to British farms and helps to signpost quality, British food.

Although the business and financial areas are vital to the farm's welfare, Chris thinks the fun side of farming is just as important. "My brother and I like to start the day with a laugh," he says. "Everybody we deal with is considered a friend. We are lucky to be in that situation."

At harvest time, the beets are mechanically lifted early morning, when the tops are standing smartly, making cutting easier. They combine harvest in the afternoons, then grade the beets in the evening. They use an outside factory for the cooking and packing for sale.

Beetroot, with its distinctive deep red colour, is considered extremely beneficial for good health, especially the eyes. It is also a little-known fact that beetroot is also thought to be an aphrodisiac. This has caused some amusement in the Moore household, especially when sales were boosted following a Yorkshire Post headline claiming 'Beetroot is the new Viagra!' Chris first spotted a wall painting that included a beetroot on a wall in Pompeii, and followed up the story and its origins from there.

Chris and his beetroot have also taken part in the long-standing TV show Come Dine With Me. He won his section with his interesting beetroot menu: beetroot bhaji, steak with beetroot and potato mash, beetroot ice cream and beetroot muffins, as well as a top tip for a tipple using the vegetable: "Simply put a frozen baby beetroot at the bottom of a brandy and champagne cocktail, to make it a really pretty pink", says Chris.

Beetroot has helped Chris in other ways too. He has been named sexiest farmer of the north on more than one occasion… beetroot anyone?

Green Pea SOUP
with PANCETTA CREAM and Soda Bread

Serves: 6 // Preparation and cooking time: 1 hour

INGREDIENTS

For the soda bread
170g self-raising flour
170g plain flour
½ tsp salt
1 tsp dried thyme
1 tsp bicarbonate of soda
300ml buttermilk

For the soup
30g butter
1 large onion, peeled
   and chopped
1 small potato, peeled
   and finely chopped
1 clove garlic, peeled
   and chopped
1 litre chicken or
   vegetable stock
500g frozen peas
1 tbsp chopped parsley
½ tbsp chopped mint
100ml double cream
sea salt and freshly
   ground black pepper
a little grated nutmeg

For the pancetta cream
15g butter
1 clove garlic, peeled
   and finely chopped
2 shallots, finely chopped
110g pancetta, finely diced
50ml white wine
200ml whipping cream
sea salt and freshly
   ground black pepper

METHOD

1. Preheat the oven to 200°C/ fan 180°C/400°F/gas mark 6.

2. For the soda bread: put both of the flours, salt, thyme and bicarbonate of soda into a large mixing bowl and mix together.

3. Make a well in the centre and pour in the buttermilk, mixing quickly with a large knife to form a soft dough. Turn onto a lightly-floured surface and briefly knead. Form into a large ball and flatten the dough slightly before placing on a lightly floured baking sheet. Cut a cross on the top and bake for approximately 20–30 minutes or until the loaf sounds hollow when tapped. Cool on a wire rack and serve with the soup.

4. To make the soup: heat the butter or oil in a heavy-based saucepan over a medium heat, add the onion, potato and garlic and sweat for 3–4 minutes until the vegetables are soft.

5. Add the stock and simmer for 8 minutes until the potato is soft.

6. Add the peas, parsley and mint and cook for a further 5 minutes until the peas are just cooked.

7. Add the cream and blend the soup until smooth, seasoning with sea salt, black pepper and a little nutmeg.

8. To make the pancetta cream: melt the butter over a medium heat and sweat the garlic and shallots for 3–4 minutes until soft.

9. Add the pancetta and cook for a further 2 minutes.

10. Add the wine and cook, stirring until most of the liquid has reduced, stir in the cream and bring to the boil.

11. Reduce the heat and simmer gently, stirring often for about 3 minutes, or until slightly thickened; season to taste.

12. Serve the soup in a warm bowl topped with the pancetta cream, crispy pancetta and soda bread.

Citrus, Beetroot and BABY KALE SALAD

Serves: 4 // Preparation time: 10 minutes // Cooking time: 10 minutes

INGREDIENTS

For the salad
140g baby kale, spinach,
   or spring green mix
1 ripe blood orange,
   peeled and sectioned
1 ripe grapefruit, peeled
   and sectioned
125g Gorgonzola
   cheese, crumbled
100g walnuts, roughly
   chopped
200g pack of beetroot,
   roughly chopped

For the dressing
3 tbsp olive oil
2 tbsp red wine vinegar
1 tbsp maple syrup
2 tsp Dijon mustard
6 sage leaves, chopped
a pinch of salt

METHOD

1. Wash and pat dry the baby kale
   and place in a large salad bowl.

2. Combine all the salad ingredients
   with the kale, sprinkling the
   Gorgonzola cheese intermittently.

3. Mix together all the dressing
   ingredients and drizzle over the
   salad, tossing until well coated.

TOP
TIP

A screw-top jar works well for mixing together salad dressings.

MEET 𝓉𝒽𝑒 FARMER

Alastair Wilson

Meet Alastair Wilson whose farm sits high above sea level near Merseyside, second generation farmer since 1972; he's hoping the third generation will eventually take over from him.

Alastair grows a lovely selection of vegetables in Rainford, sitting on moss or bog land, and he thinks it may well be the highest farm of this type in the country. His produce includes salad leaves, carrots, leeks, cabbage, Brussels sprouts and broccoli, and the land is minimally tilled, which is a conservation system used by some farmers to see a minimum disturbance of the soil to grow crops.

He has always had a passion for farming, for its lifestyle, the countryside, working with mates in the team, and trying to work with weather – whatever it might throw at them.

"Sensible people wouldn't do it, but I love the buzz when it all goes well," he laughs. "I like the idea that we are helping to feed a nation. And I want people to be excited about eating great British veg."

In summer, the hard work starts early in the morning, dealing with emails and orders, checking how the staff are doing, making sure irrigation is working when needed and maintaining machinery. It is a constant wheel of activity.

Like many vegetable growers Alastair harvests crops all year round with a peak season from May to October. As he's not able to fulfil his workforce needs locally he looks to supply people from overseas. With more than 100 workers needed on farm during this peak season he says he's finding it more difficult to employ people from agencies in these uncertain times. Because there are fewer workers available, the vacancies are easy for them to come by. Those that do come need training; all in all a challenge.

Alastair is happy after a busy day to come back to a shredded ham joint, accompanied by new potatoes and some of his flavoursome cabbage and carrots!

Aromatic STUFFED TOMATOES

Serves: 2 // Preparation time: 5 minutes // Cooking time: 20 minutes

INGREDIENTS

4 beef tomatoes
25g butter
1 medium onion, peeled
   and finely chopped
1 small clove garlic,
   peeled and crushed
1 stick celery, finely chopped
40g fresh wholemeal
   breadcrumbs
1 tbsp chopped fresh herbs,
   eg basil, oregano, marjoram
seasoning to taste

METHOD

1. Preheat oven to 180°C/
   fan 160°C/325°F/gas mark 4.

2. Stand the tomatoes on their stem ends
   and slice off the top quarter. Remove
   and reserve the tomato pulp. Turn
   the tomatoes upside down to drain.

3. Melt the butter in a pan and fry the
   onion, garlic and celery until soft, but
   not browned. Stir in the breadcrumbs,
   herbs and tomato pulp. Season well.

4. Fill the tomato cases with the mixture
   and replace the tops. Place the tomatoes
   in an ovenproof dish and bake in the
   oven for 20 minutes. Serve hot.

TOP TIP
To give the filling a crispy and golden top, remove the tomato lids and place them in
the base of the dish halfway through the cooking time.

RUNNER BEAN
RISOTTO
with *Smoked Haddock*

Serves: 4 // Preparation time: 15 minutes // Cooking time: 30 minutes

INGREDIENTS

4 tbsp olive oil
1 medium onion,
  finely chopped
400g smoked haddock,
  skinned and de-boned
300ml double cream
300g risotto rice
1 small glass of white wine
1 litre hot chicken
  or fish stock
200g fresh runner
  beans, shredded
50g grated Parmesan
salt and freshly ground
  black pepper to taste

METHOD

1. Preheat the oven to 200°C/
   fan 180°C/400°F/gas mark 6.

2. In a large saucepan heat the oil and then add
   the onion and sweat for 8 minutes until soft,
   without colouring, stirring occasionally.

3. Meanwhile, put the haddock and cream in a
   small baking tray and cover with tin foil. Place
   in the top of the oven for 10–12 minutes until
   cooked, remove from the oven and keep warm.

4. Meanwhile, add the rice to the onions and continue
   to stir until the rice has turned translucent.

5. Now add the wine. When the mixture has
   reduced, slowly add the hot stock, a little at a
   time, stirring occasionally to avoid sticking.

6. When nearly all of the stock has gone or
   the rice is almost cooked, add the runner
   beans and cook for a further 2 minutes.

7. When the rice is cooked, break up the
   haddock slightly and then stir into the
   rice with the cream. The haddock should
   break up a little more as you stir.

8. Now turn off the heat and add nearly all of the
   Parmesan and season with salt and pepper. Serve
   with the remaining Parmesan sprinkled over the top.

SEARED LAMB CHOPS with MINTED Summer Beans

Serves: 4 // Preparation time: 30 minutes // Cooking time: 6 minutes

INGREDIENTS

8 lamb chops
1 tbsp oil
1 tsp dried oregano
2 tsp lemon juice
salt and freshly ground
  black pepper
175g runner beans,
  trimmed and sliced
175g shelled broad beans
175g green beans, trimmed

For the dressing
6 tbsp olive oil
2 tbsp lemon juice
3 tbsp fresh mint,
  finely chopped
1 tsp sugar
1 tsp Dijon mustard

METHOD

1. Place the chops in a shallow dish.

2. Mix together the oil, oregano and
   lemon juice and pour over the
   chops. Season with salt and pepper.
   Cover and leave for 30 minutes.

3. Heat a cast-iron skillet or griddle until
   very hot and place the chops on the hot
   surface. Cook for 3–6 minutes on each
   side, depending on the thickness of the
   chops and how well done you like them.

4. Cook all the beans in a pan of lightly
   salted boiling water for 3–4 minutes
   or until just tender. Drain well.

5. Place all the dressing ingredients into a
   screw-top jar and shake until blended.
   Season to taste. Pour nearly all the
   dressing over the hot beans and toss.

6. Serve the chops and beans on
   warmed plates with the remaining
   dressing poured over the top.

Pork, CHERRY and PISTACHIO TERRINE

Serves: 10–12 // Preparation time: 20 minutes // Cooking time: 1 hour

INGREDIENTS

1 tbsp olive oil
15g unsalted butter
1 large onion, peeled
    and diced
2 tbsp Cognac
1 tsp fennel seeds
1 large chicken breast
750g lean pork mince
75g cherries, pitted
    and cut into eighths
2 tbsp parsley,
    finely chopped
25g pistachios, shelled
    and roughly chopped
salt and freshly
    ground pepper
14 rashers unsmoked
    bacon, stretched
    with the back of a
    cook's knife until
    half as long again

METHOD

1. Preheat the oven to 180°C/ fan 160°C/350°F/gas mark 4.

2. In a frying pan, add the olive oil and butter and melt.

3. Add the onion and soften until translucent (4–5 minutes). When softened, remove from the heat and allow to cool to room temperature.

4. Deglaze the pan with the Cognac and cook for 30 seconds, then add to the onions.

5. In a dry pan toast the fennel seeds for 1–2 minutes on a medium-low heat until they start to release their aromas. Remove from the heat and grind in a spice blender or pestle and mortar until powder.

6. In a food processor, blitz the chicken breast until minced well.

7. In a large mixing bowl, add the chicken, pork mince, cherries, onion, Cognac, fennel seeds, parsley, pistachios, and season well with salt and pepper.

8. Using your hands, mix well so that everything is combined equally.

9. Line the bottom of a 900g loaf tin with a piece of greaseproof paper. Then line the tin with the bacon so half the bacon is in the tin and the other half hanging, as you'll need to wrap this over the top to make sure the top of the terrine is covered.

10. Add the terrine mixture then fold over the bacon to seal the top of the terrine. Cover with a piece of greased foil.

11. Boil a kettle. Place the terrine tin in a roasting tin, and then pour the boiling water into the tin so it comes up half-way, and place the tin into the oven. Cook for 1 hour or just over, so it is cooked all the way through and juices run clear when pierced in the centre with a knife.

12. Remove the tin from the oven when cooked. Take the terrine tin out of the roasting tray and allow to cool to room temperature. Chill well, overnight if you have time, before removing from the mould, peeling off the lining paper and slicing.

13. Serve with crusty bread and dressed salad leaves (optional).

Roly Holt

Meet the Holts. Roly and his mother Laura are part of a family farming business growing tomatoes in an area covering the equivalent of around 22 football pitches.

The family started their business in the late 1970s with one nursery. Roly's father Rick formed the original farm, and was joined by Roly and his sister Felicity. They now have three nurseries where they grow speciality tomatoes in glasshouses for some of the country's largest retailers as well as supplying local farm shops. Using innovative and sustainable methods is one of the core principles of the farming enterprise as Roly explains.

"Tomato growing is not just growing tomatoes; it is a very technical business. From utilising the modern glass structures with computer-controlled equipment to ensuring the whole farm is energy efficient. Energy is a very important part of our business and we have implemented a lot of new technology to ensure we maximise its use and remain as efficient as possible, including modern gas Combined Heat and Power (CHP) Systems, Biomass, Biomass CHP, solar and carbon dioxide from anaerobic digestion units, where waste is used to produce fuel."

A typical day is spent mainly between the three sites looking at the crops and checking the growing climate – necessary because every day is different here in the UK. There are also many visitors to the site, from crop consultants to children from local schools who visit to find out more about where their food comes from.

The farm also hosts farmers from farther afield, such as China, Japan and Australia, to share best practice and lessons learned from the farm.

Despite Holt's nurseries growing around 400,000 tomato plants a year – which produce around 150 million tomatoes – the UK remains only 20% self-sufficient in home-grown tomatoes, with the rest being made up of imports.

Roly says: "In the peak season, typically running from April to September, it's all hands on deck to keep up with picking the crop with cherry tomatoes, on the vine, cocktail, classic and baby plums all being grown. And the drive to remain efficient and improve quality means the business is extremely varied which brings its own challenges. Tomatoes are a really fast-growing crop with a long season and every day brings up new obstacles to overcome. Being able to address those and improve for future seasons is a good challenge to have. I am really proud of our recent introduction of LED lighting as this has enabled us to grow tomatoes all through the year. Producing them every day of the year is great for our business and the end customer who has more access to this great British crop."

With Roly's favourite British dish being fish and chips with plenty of tomato ketchup there is bound to be some of his tomatoes adding flavour.

R&L HOLT

ENGLISH TOMATOES

R&L HOLT

ENGLISH TOMATOES

Roasted BROCCOLI and CAULIFLOWER with Lemon and Garlic

Serves: 5 // Preparation time: 10 minutes // Cooking time: 30 minutes

INGREDIENTS

1 head of broccoli, broken
   into small florets
1 large head of cauliflower,
   broken into small florets
3 tbsp olive oil
4 garlic cloves, sliced thinly
2 lemons, sliced thinly
salt and freshly ground
   black pepper to taste

METHOD

1. Preheat the oven to 220°C/
   fan 200°C/425°F/gas mark 7.

2. Mix all of the ingredients in a
   large bowl until coated in the oil.
   Tip them out onto a baking tray
   (you may need two).

3. Roast in the oven for 25–30
   minutes, tossing the vegetables
   halfway through the cooking
   time. Remove from the oven once
   they are brown and tender.

4. Serve hot.

TOP TIP Sprinkle over a generous helping of nutmeg, salt and pepper to add a note of spiciness and warmth.

CAJUN *Chicken* BURGER

Serves: 4 // Preparation time: 15 minutes // Cooking time: 20 minutes

INGREDIENTS

For the guacamole
3 avocados, finely chopped
8 tomatoes, finely chopped
1 red onion, finely chopped
3 tbsp white wine vinegar
8 mint leaves, chopped
handful of freshly
 chopped coriander
3 red chillies, deseeded
 and finely chopped
4 cloves of garlic
 finely chopped

For the filling
4 small chicken breasts
a little flour
2 tsp Cajun spices
1 tsp smoked garlic powder
few good pinches of
 smoked paprika
2–3 eggs, beaten
crispy breadcrumbs, either
 panko or dried breadcrumbs
butter or oil for frying
4 large buns
1 lettuce
1 small tub sour cream
8 slices chorizo
2 balls mozzarella cut
 into thin slices

METHOD

1. First make the guacamole by mixing all the ingredients together and refrigerate.

2. Slightly flatten the chicken breasts. Mix the flour, Cajun spice, garlic powder and smoked paprika together and coat the breasts with the mix, shaking off any excess.

3. Dip the chicken breasts in beaten egg, then in breadcrumbs, and fry in a little butter and oil or just oil for about 15–20 minutes depending on the thickness of chicken. Test with a knife to make sure there are no pink juices coming out. If in doubt finish in an oven on a baking sheet.

4. To assemble, place a large lettuce leaf in a bun, top with a spoonful of sour cream, followed by a chicken breast, two chorizo slices, some slices of mozzarella and finally a spoonful of guacamole.

5. Repeat until all the buns are filled.

BEEF KEBABS
with Courgette, Pepper and ROSEMARY

Serves: 4 // Preparation and cooking time: 30 minutes

INGREDIENTS

500g beef fillet, trimmed
   of excess skin
2 medium courgettes, diced
1 large orange pepper, cored,
   deseeded, and chopped
1 large red pepper, cored,
   seeded and chopped
2 large garlic cloves, minced
100ml olive oil
1–2 rosemary sprigs, leaves
   chopped, plus extra
   to garnish
salt and freshly ground
   black pepper

METHOD

1. Preheat the grill or a barbecue to a moderately hot temperature.

2. Cut the beef fillet into bite-sized chunks.

3. Thread the beef, courgette, and peppers onto four metal skewers, alternating them. Arrange end-to-end in a large rectangular baking dish.

4. Stir together the garlic, olive oil, and chopped rosemary in a small mixing bowl. Brush the mixture all over the kebabs.

5. Place under the grill or on the barbecue. Cook until the beef is firm to the touch yet slightly springy, and the vegetables are lightly charred, about 6–8 minutes; turn from time to time.

6. Remove from the heat and let rest for 5 minutes before serving with a garnish of rosemary.

TOMATO *Tarte* TATIN

Serves: 6 // Preparation time: 20 minutes // Cooking time: 30 minutes

INGREDIENTS

225g plain flour
1 heaped tsp baking powder
salt and freshly ground
    black pepper
50g butter, cubed
150ml semi-skimmed milk
2 tbsp olive oil
700g heritage tomatoes,
    halved or quartered if
    large, or other good-
    flavoured vine tomatoes
1 tsp freshly chopped
    basil, plus 8 fresh basil
    leaves, torn, to garnish
2 tsp balsamic vinegar

METHOD

1. Sieve the flour and baking powder
   into a large bowl and season.

2. Rub in the butter using
   just your fingertips.

3. Add the milk to make a soft
   dough and set aside.

4. Preheat the oven to 220°C/
   fan 200°C/425°F/gas mark 7.

5. Pour the oil into a shallow,
   24cm round ovenproof dish. Lay the
   tomatoes on the bottom of the dish,
   sprinkle over the chopped basil and
   balsamic vinegar and season.

6. Roll the dough out to fit over the
   tomatoes, place over the top and tuck
   the edges inside the dish to seal.

7. Cook in the oven for about 30 minutes
   until the crust is well risen and golden.

8. Remove from the oven and release
   the edges with a knife. Leave to
   cool for 4 minutes and then turn
   upside down onto a serving dish.

9. Scatter over the fresh basil
   and serve warm.

Tomato and PEPPER PENNE Pasta

Serves: 4 // Preparation time: 15 minutes // Cooking time: 25–30 minutes

INGREDIENTS

4 different coloured peppers,
    quartered and deseeded
700g tomatoes, halved if large
85g walnut halves
3 garlic cloves, sliced
small bunch of fresh basil
3 tbsp olive oil
1 tbsp balsamic vinegar
salt and freshly ground
    black pepper

To finish

400g penne or macaroni
    dried pasta
40g butter
fresh basil, to garnish
Parmesan cheese, grated,
    to garnish

METHOD

1. Preheat the oven to 190°C/fan 170°C/375°F/ gas mark 5.

2. Arrange the peppers with the skin sides uppermost in a roasting tin; add the tomatoes, walnut halves and garlic and tear the basil over the top.

3. Drizzle with the oil and vinegar and season. Roast for 25–30 minutes until the peppers are browned.

4. When the vegetables are almost ready, bring a large saucepan of water to the boil, add the pasta and cook for 8–10 minutes or according to the packet directions until just tender.

5. Scoop the vegetables out of the roasting tin, reserving the pan juices. Remove the pepper and tomato skins with a knife and fork and then slice the peppers and roughly chop the tomatoes and walnuts.

6. Drain the pasta, return to the empty pan and toss with the butter and a little extra seasoning. Stir in the roasted vegetables and nuts and reserved pan juices.

7. Spoon into bowls and top with extra basil leaves, a drizzle of olive oil and a little Parmesan.

TOP TIP

These roasted vegetables are just as good added to cooked puy lentils, bulgar wheat or couscous instead of pasta. Serve hot or leave to cool and add to salad leaves.

MEET the FARMER

Bal Padda

A community-spirited soft fruit grower from the Vale of Evesham – meet Bal Padda, who marries Punjabi and UK values in a diverse environment.

Bal Padda is a second generation soft fruit grower, specialising in strawberries and raspberries. His father, Makhan Singh Padda, emigrated to England from the Punjab and set up the business in 1996 as a one-man operation in Worcestershire's beautiful Vale of Evesham. He and his son now work together, employing 12 full-time staff and over 200 seasonal workers.

The farm grows fruit in polytunnels to mitigate the vagaries of weather and birds. The fruit is grown for most of the year, apart from six weeks in the winter, when the team spends its time maintaining the polytunnels and general work on the farm. Bal opted to not have pick your own and instead sells all his produce to the UK market. In the picking season, his day starts with his staff very early at 4.30am in the cool of the morning. His teams, most living on site and from Europe, work early on and then go home during the hottest part of the day, as the heat in the tunnels can become very high, before returning in the evening to finish picking for the day.

"I am not your typical British farmer," Bal says with a smile. "My family comes from a part of India that is considered the bread basket of the country, so I like to think we are reflecting that vision of food provision over here. My father still gives out this wonderful Punjabi image –

he's a six foot tall turbaned man – but working and living in a very English environment, even in the iconically-named Vicarage Nurseries.

"I love working in the fresh air, literally seeing the fruits of our labour. I like to give something back to the community and so, some time ago, we founded Growers United FC (GUFC), raising funds for charity and for the community. It's a really proactive initiative that offers football matches, golf days and dinners to around 32 other farms in the area, who get involved and provide teams of all different nationalities; celebrity names get involved too. We want to show that racism is not an option – we strive to make the future better for all our children rather than harping on about the past. We are part of the 'Show Racism the Red Card' movement."

So far, their charitable activities have raised over £100,000, given to Birmingham Children's Hospital, Cancer Research UK and local charities; this year they helped Show Racism The Red Card too.

Asked whether he enjoys his own fruit, Bal says that he rarely has time to eat them, although his partner does make delicious jams. However, Bal does make time for his favourite British dish: a fish-finger sandwich!

SUMMER PUDDING

Serves: 6 // Preparation time: 30 minutes // Chilling time: 12 hours

INGREDIENTS

675–900g summer fruits
  (eg strawberries,
  raspberries, blackcurrants,
  redcurrants)
2–3 tbsp caster sugar
2 packets of sponge fingers
4–6 tbsp sherry or
  Madeira or port
1 tub double cream,
  whipped stiffly, or
  thick crème fraîche

METHOD

1. If you are using red or blackcurrants, damsons or plums, you need to cook these first with the sugar, stirring occasionally, and adding the raspberries or strawberries after these harder fruits have begun to soften (about 5 minutes). When all the fruit is softened, drain (reserving the liquid) and cool.

2. Use a pretty straight-edged glass trifle bowl with straight sides. Dip each sponge finger into the sherry and use them to layer the bottom of the dish. Now work your way around the edges of the bowl, standing each finger upright like a soldier. Don't dip the fingers in for too long otherwise they go soggy.

3. Pour in the fruit mixture and make a final layer of fingers on top. Spoon over any juices from the fruit, so that most of the fingers are coloured up. Place some cling film over the top and place a plate over the fingers with a heavy weight on top (a tin of tomatoes will do!). Place in the fridge overnight.

4. As this version of summer pudding is not turned out as the ones with bread are, you can decorate the top with cream and people get a nice surprise when they see the pudding opened.

STRAWBERRY Trifle with PIMM'S

Serves: 6 // Preparation time: 25 minutes // Chilling time: 2 hours

INGREDIENTS

4 trifle sponges, about
   100g in total
350g British strawberries,
   sliced
4 tbsp caster sugar
4 tbsp Pimm's, undiluted
425g can of reduced
   fat custard
200ml double cream
150g low-fat natural yoghurt
grated rind of half a orange
grated rind of half a lemon
3 strawberries, halved and
   a few tiny pansy flowers
   or lemon and orange
   rind curls to decorate

METHOD

1. Break the trifle sponges into pieces
   and arrange in a single layer in
   the base of a 1.2 litre glass dish.

2. Arrange the strawberries on top,
   sprinkle with 2 tablespoons of the
   sugar, then spoon over the Pimm's.

3. Spoon the custard over the
   top of the fruit and spread the
   top into an even layer.

4. Whip the cream in a bowl until it just
   forms soft swirls then fold in the yoghurt
   and fruit rinds. Spoon this mixture over
   the custard layer and chill until required.

5. Decorate with the halved strawberries
   and pansy flowers or lemon and
   orange rind curls made with a
   zester just before serving.

TOP TIP Look for the Red Tractor logo when shopping for your ingredients to ensure you are buying quality British produce.

STRAWBERRY *and* RASPBERRY *Ripple* ═══ ETON MESS ═══

Serves: 6 // Preparation time: 35 minutes // Cooking time: 75–90 minutes

INGREDIENTS

225g strawberries, hulled
100g raspberries

For the meringues
2 egg whites
100g caster sugar

To finish
300ml double cream
200g low-fat
  fromage frais
225g strawberries,
  hulled, roughly
  chopped
50g raspberries

METHOD

1. Preheat the oven to 110°C/ fan 90°C/225°F/gas mark ¼.

2. Line a large baking sheet with non-stick baking paper.

3. Purée the strawberries and raspberries in a liquidiser or food processor then press through a sieve.

4. Whisk the egg whites in a large clean dry bowl until they form stiff moist-looking peaks and you feel confident that if the bowl was turned upside down the egg whites wouldn't fall out!

5. Gradually whisk in the sugar a teaspoonful at a time, then continue whisking for a minute or two until really thick and glossy.

6. Add 2 tablespoons of the berry purée, then very briefly mix until marbled.

7. Spoon into a large piping bag fitted with a 1.5cm plain piping tube. Pipe small rounds onto the lined baking sheet.

8. Bake for 1¼–1½ hours or until the meringues can be easily lifted off the paper. Leave to cool.

9. To serve, lightly whip the cream until it forms soft swirls, then fold in the fromage frais.

10. Crumble the meringues, then layer in jam jars or plastic containers with the remaining berry purée and diced strawberries. Decorate with the raspberries Add the lids and keep in the fridge until ready to serve or transport to a picnic in a cool bag with a frozen ice block to keep them cold. Serve within 1½ hours or the meringues tend to lose their crunch.

TOP TIP Make up the strawberry swirled meringues and fruit purée the day before, then just layer with whipped cream and extra fruit in clean recycled jam jars and screw on the lids. Take out to the garden in a basket or pack into a cool box for a picnic pud.

AUTUMN

Hay bales signal the harvest is done and
as autumn bites we tuck into hearty bakes

CAULIFLOWER *and* CHEESE
Soup with SESAME TOAST

Serves: 2 // Preparation time: 15 minutes // Cooking time: 15 minutes

INGREDIENTS

1 small cauliflower, trimmed
   (discarding rough stalks),
   washed and finely chopped
1 large potato, peeled
   and finely chopped
   into 2cm pieces
2 garlic cloves, peeled
   and finely chopped
850ml milk
25g butter
175g mature Cheddar cheese
sea salt and freshly ground
   black pepper to taste

For the sesame toast
4 slices French bread
100g sesame seeds
small amount of olive oil

METHOD

1. Put the cauliflower, potato and garlic
   in a large pan, cover with the milk and
   put on a low heat. Simmer until the
   potato is very soft, which should take
   approximately 10–12 minutes.

2. When the vegetables are cooked, add the
   butter and the cheese and, using a stick
   blender, blend until the soup is totally
   smooth. Season to taste. Set the soup
   aside somewhere warm.

3. Toast the bread slices, then drizzle some
   olive oil all over them, and sprinkle the
   sesame seeds on top.

4. Serve the soup in warm bowls with the
   sesame toast.

  TOP TIP Look for the Red Tractor logo when shopping for your ingredients to ensure you are buying quality British produce.

CREAM OF Butternut Squash soup With BREAD

Serves: 4 // Preparation and cooking time: 55 minutes

INGREDIENTS

2 tbsp olive oil, plus
   extra to serve
1 medium onion, diced
2 garlic cloves, minced
1 tbsp fresh ginger,
   peeled and grated
1 pinch paprika, plus
   extra to serve
1 large carrot, peeled
   and diced
600g butternut squash,
   peeled, seeded, and
   cut into cubes
1.2 litres chicken stock
120ml double cream,
   plus extra to serve
crusty bread slices, to serve
salt and freshly ground
   black pepper to taste

METHOD

1. Heat the olive oil in a
   large saucepan set over a
   medium heat. Add the onion,
   garlic, and a pinch of salt,
   sweating until softened,
   for about 6 minutes.

2. Add the grated ginger,
   paprika, carrot, and
   butternut squash,
   stirring well to mix.

3. Cover with the stock and
   bring to the boil. Reduce
   to a simmer and cook,
   partially covered, for
   about 20–25 minutes or
   until squash is very tender
   to the tip of a knife.

4. Remove soup from the heat
   and let cool slightly before
   puréeing with a hand blender
   until smooth; alternatively,
   you can purée in batches in
   a blender or food processor.

5. Return the soup to a simmer
   and stir in the cream. Adjust
   seasoning to taste with salt
   and pepper as needed.

6. Ladle into warm serving
   bowls and drizzle with
   some cream and a little
   olive oil. Garnish with
   some paprika and freshly
   ground black pepper
   before serving, if desired.

7. Serve with good crusty
   bread on the side.

TOP TIP   You can substitute the chicken stock with vegetable stock.

MEET ᴛʜᴇ FARMER

Jacob Anthony

Jacob Anthony comes from a long line of Welsh cattle and sheep farmers. You will find him happily working on his tractor, and sometimes taking in the breath-taking views of Somerset and Devon.

Jacob is 24 years old and a fifth generation farmer on his family farm, based in the beautiful South Wales valleys. His father, and grandfather at the ripe old age of 85, still work on Cwm Risca Farm, which has been in the family since 1926. He is a young man full of passion about running the farm in a productive and sustainable manner to continue in the manner of his forebears.

The farm is 700 acres, all in one block; it is 450ft above sea level at the yard and rises up to 850ft at the highest point. Not only does the area get an average of 80 inches of rainfall a year, but they also have to combat severe winds blowing in off the estuary.

"My love of farming has been unprecedented, ever since I could walk and talk," Jacob says proudly. "It's all I've ever wanted to do and I have had no desire to know anything different. Farming is in my blood and to me it's a way of life, not just a job. Starting each day, I have one priority: the early morning check of all the livestock.

Animal welfare is at the heart of everything we do on our farm."

His flock of Lleyn x Texel ewes produce lambs pasture-finished on grass and clover leys to produce a tender and tasty meat. The majority of the lambs are sold to Dunbia through the Wales Federation of Young Farmers' Club initiative, with the bulk of these ending up on a Sainsbury's shelf under the highly recognisable banner of PGI Welsh lamb. They also raise a commercial herd of Welsh Black x Lim Suckler cattle, with the young stock also finished on the farm.

"I don't think you can beat a traditional roast leg of succulent Welsh lamb," Jacob says. "I love mine slow-roasted and served with buttered leeks, plus a medley of fresh vegetables and crispy roast potatoes – especially if someone makes it for me! I can, however, barbecue a delicious lamb burger bursting with flavour and a texture that melts in the mouth – fantastic whatever the weather, whatever the occasion."

Beetroot Salad with APPLE and FETA CHEESE

Serves: 4 // Preparation time: 5 minutes // Cooking time: 1 hour 10 minutes

INGREDIENTS

4 medium beetroots,
  scrubbed
2 large Golden Delicious
  or Granny Smith apples,
  cored and diced
75g rocket, washed
175g feta-style cheese, cubed
4 tbsp extra-virgin olive oil
2 tbsp cider vinegar
salt and freshly ground
  black pepper to taste

METHOD

1. Preheat the oven to 180°C/
   fan 160°C/350°F/gas mark 4.

2. Individually wrap the beetroots in
   sheets of aluminium foil. Place on a
   baking tray and roast for about 1 hour
   until tender to the tip of a knife.

3. Remove from the oven and let
   cool briefly before unwrapping.
   Peel away the skins; use food safety
   gloves to prevent staining.

4. Cut into thin slices either on a
   mandoline or with a sharp knife.

5. Toss the beetroot slices with the
   apple, rocket, feta, extra-virgin
   olive oil, cider vinegar, and some
   salt and pepper to taste.

6. Divide between plates or salad
   bowls before serving.

TOP TIP Look for the Red Tractor logo when shopping for your ingredients to ensure you are buying quality British produce.

Tasty CHICKEN
TANDOORI

Serves: 4 // Preparation time: 20 minutes
// Marinade time: 4–5 hours // Cooking time: 25–35 minutes

INGREDIENTS

4 large chicken breasts, each
    cut into four pieces

Marinade
1 piece ginger, peeled
    and grated
3 cloves garlic, finely chopped
3 medium hot chillies,
    finely chopped
1 large pot natural yoghurt
half a jar of tandoori paste
2 tbsp tandoori BBQ
    masala spice blend
salt to taste

To serve
2 tbsp freshly chopped
    coriander

Raita
1 small pot natural yoghurt
1 tbsp freshly chopped mint
salt to taste

METHOD

1. For the marinade: mix together the
   ginger, garlic cloves, chillies, yoghurt,
   tandoori paste and spice blend in a bowl.

2. Add the chicken pieces to the marinade,
   stir until well covered, and leave,
   covered, for 4–5 hours or overnight.

3. Preheat the oven to 180°C/
   fan 160°C/350°F/gas mark 4.

4. Place the chicken in the marinade into
   a roasting pan and cook for 25–30
   minutes. Make sure the chicken is cooked
   by inserting a skewer into a piece – the
   juices should run clear.

5. Sprinkle with the coriander and serve
   with a salad and the raita.

TOP TIP Tandoori pastes and spice blends can be found in the
'World Foods' section of most supermarkets.

Warm LAMB and NOODLE Salad

Serves: 4 // Preparation time: 15 minutes // Cooking time: 10 minutes

INGREDIENTS

4 lean lamb leg or rump steaks
salt and freshly ground
    black pepper
2 tsp Chinese
    five-spice powder
4 tbsp sweet chilli sauce
2 tbsp plum or damson
    jam, softened with a
    little hot water
2 tbsp sunflower oil
1 tbsp sesame seeds
300g cooked egg or rice
    noodles, to serve

For the salad
100g mixed salad leaves
175g fresh radishes, sliced
1 small red onion, peeled,
    halved and thinly sliced
3 tbsp extra virgin olive oil

METHOD

1. Place the steaks on a chopping board and season on both sides with the salt, pepper and Chinese five-spice powder.

2. Place the salad ingredients into a large bowl, season and drizzle with the olive oil.

3. In a small bowl, mix together the sweet chilli sauce and plum or damson jam.

4. Heat the oil in a large, non-stick wok or frying pan. Add the lamb and cook for 4–6 minutes on each side until cooked. Halfway through cooking, add the sesame seeds. Remove the lamb from the pan, transfer to a plate to rest for 2–3 minutes, then slice into strips.

5. Arrange the warmed noodles on a serving plate and add the salad, then arrange the lamb on top. Spoon over the sweet chilli dressing and serve immediately.

 TOP TIP Look for the Red Tractor logo when shopping for your ingredients to ensure you are buying quality British produce.

Baked APPLES
with HAM and CRANBERRY

Serves: 4 // Preparation and cooking time: 1 hour 10 minutes

INGREDIENTS

2 tbsp unsalted butter, cubed,
   plus extra to serve
1 large onion, finely sliced
1 large red cabbage, shredded
3–4 bay leaves
2 tsp caraway seeds
100ml red wine vinegar
100ml water
4 large Cox apples
750g ham or gammon
   joint, trimmed of
   excess fat and diced
225g cranberries
salt and freshly ground
   black pepper

METHOD

1. Melt the butter in a
   large saucepan set over
   a medium heat. Add the
   onion and a pinch of salt,
   sweating until just softened
   for about 5 minutes.

2. Stir in the cabbage, bay
   leaves, caraway seeds,
   red wine vinegar, water,
   and some salt and freshly
   ground black pepper.

3. Cover and cook over a
   medium-low heat, stirring
   occasionally, until the
   cabbage is very soft, about
   45 minutes.

4. In the meantime, remove
   the tops of the apples, and
   place to one side. Hollow out
   the apples, leaving enough
   space to stuff with the filling.

5. Toss the diced ham and
   cranberries with some
   salt and pepper to taste
   in a mixing bowl.

6. Preheat the oven to 180°C/
   fan 160°C/350°F/gas mark 4.

7. When the cabbage is
   ready, spoon into a large
   baking dish. Arrange the
   apples among the cabbage
   and fill with the ham and
   cranberry mixture.

8. Replace the tops of the
   apples over the filling and
   dot with some butter.

9. Cover the dish with a sheet
   of aluminium foil. Bake for 1
   hour, removing the foil after
   30 minutes, until the apples
   are soft to the tip of a knife.

10. Remove from the oven
    and let cool briefly
    before serving.

MEET ᵗʰᵉ FARMER

Anna Longthorp

Meet award-winning Anna Longthorp, who sells her fabulous free-range pork to shops and restaurants. Thank goodness the Merchant Navy missed out...

Fourth-generation farmer Anna rears pigs near Doncaster, leading her life as a busy single mum, looking after both her little boy and her free-range pigs. Her brother deals with the arable side of the farm and is also responsible for the pig enterprise. Anna grew up on the farm and has been working there full-time since joining the family business over nine years ago. She is excited about their own brand of pork, which she offers wholesale to shops, farm shops and restaurants from their butchery, making their own sausages and selling all different cuts of pork, including ham and bacon.

The pigs are a Landrace x Duroc x Pietrain breed, living happily outdoors with arks; the 'mums-to-be' have their own individual arks while the rest are kept in groups in 'tents', with solid sides and canvas shelter over the top.

"No day is the same," says Anna. "Once I have dropped my little boy off at nursery, I am in and out of the office or butchery, checking or actually working there, if needs be. After I have picked up my boy at lunchtime, I like to see customers or walk around the farm with him. I love the life, and it's all I've ever known. I consider what I am doing now will be a sound future for my son."

One of her first challenges was to try and use the whole carcass of the pig, so when sales of shoulders of pork flagged, they developed recipes for pulled pork or ham, which are very popular. A customer selling pet foods takes the tails, ears and trotters, so maximum value is gained from each pig, with little waste. Now the pork brand wins awards from enterprises such as Deliciously Yorkshire.

All this might have just passed the family by had it not been for grandpa, a merchant navy man, who was told he had to stay at home on the farm rather than go back to sea when he proposed to Anna's grandmother. He developed the farm and the rest is Longthorp family history. Even Anna's other love, being a tennis coach, has had to take a back seat!

And Anna's favourite dish? "Easy," she says: "Fruity pork curry, a trusted Ladies in Pigs recipe that is just divine, a firm family favourite and has been for years."

WARM PEAR and Goats' Cheese SALAD

Serves: 4 // Preparation time: 5 minutes // Cooking time: 5 minutes

INGREDIENTS

25g butter
2 tbsp hazelnuts,
    roughly chopped
3 firm pears, peeled, cored,
    and cut into wedges
freshly ground black pepper
100g mixed salad leaves
100g mild English or
    Welsh goats' cheese

METHOD

1. Heat the butter in a small frying pan and fry the hazelnuts for 1–2 minutes until just browned.

2. Add the pears to the pan, season with a little pepper and fry for 2–3 minutes, turning once, until just golden and tender.

3. Toss the warm pear wedges into the salad leaves and arrange on four plates.

4. Crumble the cheese and scatter with the hazelnuts over the top.

  Look for the Red Tractor logo when shopping for your ingredients to ensure you are buying quality British produce.

DUCK with Hot Chillies COOL PEPPERS and APPLE RAITA

Serves: 4 // Preparation time: 10 minutes // Cooking time: 10 minutes

INGREDIENTS

1 tsp cumin seeds
2 green peppers,
    cored and sliced
3–4 tomatoes
small piece of root
    ginger, peeled and
    roughly chopped
1 onion, peeled and
    roughly chopped
1 clove garlic, peeled
    and chopped
2 hot green chillies,
    roughly chopped
1 tbsp groundnut oil or ghee
1 tbsp Gujarat Masala
    curry paste or similar
450g pack duck breast
    mini-fillets

For the raita
grated zest and juice
    of ½ lime
1 dessert apple,
    grated skin-on
150g pot natural yoghurt
1 pinch salt
1 pinch cayenne pepper

METHOD

1. Heat a large deep frying pan, add the cumin seeds and dry-fry for a few seconds. Turn them into a bowl and take the pan off the heat.

2. To make the raita, put the lime zest and juice in a bowl and toss the apple into the juice. Add the yoghurt with salt and cayenne and set to one side.

3. Place the peppers and tomatoes into a separate bowl and set aside.

4. Blend the ginger, onion, garlic, chillies and cumin seeds and then blend them to a paste with the Gujarat masala.

5. Heat the pan again, add the oil and fry the paste for 3–4 minutes over a medium heat.

6. Increase the heat, add the duck and stir-fry for 3 minutes. Add the peppers and tomatoes and cook for a further 3 minutes. Season to taste with a little more salt if needed.

7. Serve with the apple raita.

TOAD-in-the-HOLE

Serves: 4 // Preparation and cooking time: 45 minutes

INGREDIENTS

2 tbsp vegetable oil
4–5 thick pork sausages,
  at least 85% pork content,
  if possible
250g plain flour
½ tsp salt
2 large eggs
600ml whole milk

METHOD

1. Preheat the oven to 220°C/
   fan 200°C/425°F/gas mark 7.

2. Heat half the oil in a large frying pan
   set over a moderate heat. Add the
   sausages and fry for about 5 minutes,
   until browned on all sides. Set aside.

3. Heat the remaining oil in a
   large baking dish or roasting tin
   in the oven until very hot.

4. In the meantime, combine the
   flour and salt into a mixing bowl
   and make a well in the centre.

5. Break in the eggs and gradually work
   in half the milk, beating well until
   smooth. Beat in the rest of the milk.

6. Pour the batter into the preheated
   dish and arrange the sausages in it.
   Return to the oven and cook for about
   30 minutes until risen and puffy.
   Remove from the oven and let the
   dish stand briefly before serving.

TOP TIP Toad-in-the-hole works perfectly with bubble and squeak
(p.83) as an accompanying dish.

Bonfire RIBS

Serves: 8 // Preparation time: 5 minutes // Cooking time: 1 hour

INGREDIENTS

1.8kg pork spare ribs
6 tbsp tomato ketchup
4 tbsp mango chutney
3 tbsp sunflower oil
2 tbsp Worcester sauce
2 tbsp soft brown sugar
2 tbsp vinegar
freshly ground black pepper

METHOD

1. Preheat the oven to 190°C/
   fan 170°C/375°F/gas mark 5.

2. Place the ribs in a large pan, cover
   with cold water and bring to the boil.
   Boil for 5 minutes, drain well and
   transfer to a large roasting tin.

3. Blend together the remaining
   ingredients and season with black
   pepper. Brush liberally over the ribs.

4. Roast in the oven for 45 minutes to
   1 hour, turning and basting occasionally
   until the ribs are cooked through
   and slightly charred in places.

  TOP TIP Look for the Red Tractor logo when buying your ingredients to ensure you are buying quality British produce.

Individual LAMB WELLINGTONS

Serves: 4 // Preparation time: 35 minutes // Cooking time: 20 minutes

INGREDIENTS

1–2 tbsp olive oil
1 small sprig of fresh rosemary
salt and freshly ground
    black pepper
2 lean cannons of lamb (one
    half of the loin side of lamb)
    (approx. 400g), trimmed and
    cut into 4 equal portions
50g wild mushrooms, cleaned
    and finely chopped
1 shallot, peeled and
    finely chopped
1 tbsp fresh thyme leaves
75g farmhouse pâté, softened
375g pack of ready-rolled
    puff pastry sheets
1 egg, beaten
handful of fresh thyme
    leaves, to garnish

METHOD

1. Heat the oil and rosemary
   in a non-stick frying pan
   over a moderate heat.

2. Season the lamb portions
   and brown for 30 seconds on
   each side. Set aside to cool.

3. In the same pan, add
   the mushrooms, shallot
   and thyme leaves. Cook
   for 5–10 minutes until
   soft. Set aside to cool.

4. Preheat the oven to 220°C/
   fan 210°C/425°F/gas mark 7.

5. Put the lamb portions on
   a clean chopping board.
   Spread each portion
   evenly with the pâté, then
   the mushroom mixture.
   Press down lightly.

6. On a lightly floured surface,
   unroll the pastry and divide
   into eight equal squares.
   Roll four to approximately
   6cm larger than the base
   to allow for covering
   each lamb portion.

7. Position each lamb portion
   on a pastry square, leaving
   a 1cm border. Press down
   gently and brush the edges
   with some of the beaten
   egg. Place the larger pastry
   square over the lamb, neatly
   trim the edges and pinch all
   around the pastry to seal.

8. Brush the surface with the
   remaining egg and sprinkle
   with the thyme. Gently mark
   the surface of the pastry with
   the point of a sharp knife to
   allow any steam to escape.

9. Transfer the Wellingtons to
   a baking sheet and cook for
   12–15 minutes for a medium
   choice; longer for well done.
   Leave to rest for 3–4 minutes.

10. Serve with fresh, seasonal
    vegetables and boiled new
    potatoes.

MEET the FARMER

Whizz Middleton

Farming on the rolling Barton Hills in Bedfordshire and Hertfordshire, Whizz and her sister Ellie set up their rapeseed oil business, which is now award-winning.

Whizz's family has been farming in this area for hundreds of years. She grew up on the family farm, enjoying the wildlife around her on the chalk downlands. Whizz spent her childhood shadowing her father on her own little pedal tractor with a trailer which she used to rescue stranded lambs. Before long, her father taught her to drive a proper tractor and the rest is farming history.

The farm is entirely arable, bearing crops of cereals, legumes and oilseed rape. Minimum tillage combined with ploughing produces good crops which go to local merchants and Stotfold Watermill, with a small amount of rapeseed saved for their new oil enterprise set up in 2012. Following natural rapeseed, Whizz now produced flavoured oils (such as their latest basil oil), mayonnaises and salad dressings. They supply restaurants and farm shops both locally and in Cornwall where Ellie now lives. One particular restaurant in Woburn, Paris House, has worked closely with Whizz to develop two new dressings, and her and her young children Millie and George were thrilled to help choose the final versions!

'My day starts early with the family,' says Whizz, 'and is spent organising our team, seeing to orders and deliveries, meeting with finance or agronomy specialists, feeding the team during harvest time out in the fields, and generally keeping the family happy.'

Whizz is very involved in the integrated IT system on farm and uses the latest technology to help to make evidence-based decisions on how best to raise next year's crops and varieties.

'Knowing where food comes from,' continues Whizz, 'is becoming more and more important to people and the decisions they make buying food. I like how our farm is linked to the community. People become interested in farming in general the more knowledge they have, and they like to look up the grid references we put on our bottles! Organised farm walks have encouraged the interest.'

Whizz loves to know what people are using their oils for, besides the usual choices for roasting. The most unusual so far is one chef who makes rapeseed oil ice cream!

Rural crime can be a real problem in the area. Looking suspiciously like a farm thief herself one morning at 4am, Whizz laughs recounting the tale of being stopped by police when she was being rushed to hospital to have her son – they didn't delay her for long!

She and her family like to spend time enjoying their favourite Sunday lamb roast with all the trimmings, including her mother-in-law's suet pudding recipe, and her own mother's roast potatoes, cooked – of course – with their own rapeseed oil!

Baked EGGS with SPINACH

Serves: 2–4 // Preparation time: 15 minutes // Cooking time: 10–12 minutes

INGREDIENTS

450g fresh spinach,
   washed and drained
25g butter
freshly grated nutmeg
salt and freshly ground
   black pepper
4 large eggs
4 tbsp double cream
4 tbsp freshly grated
   Parmesan

METHOD

1. Preheat the oven to 190°C/
   fan 170°C/375°F/gas mark 5.

2. Tear the spinach leaves from their stalks,
   wash and place into a large pan.

3. Cook, covered, for a couple of minutes
   until the spinach has wilted.

4. Drain thoroughly, pressing out
   any excess liquid, and then return
   to the pan with half the butter,
   nutmeg and seasoning. Mix well.

5. Divide the spinach between two buttered,
   shallow gratin dishes (or four large
   ramekins). Make a well in the spinach,
   break in the eggs and season. Spoon
   over the cream. Sprinkle with Parmesan
   and dot with the remaining butter.

6. Bake for 10–12 minutes until
   the eggs are just set.

7. Serve with crusty bread to
   mop up any juices.

  TOP TIP Look for the British Lion mark when buying eggs.

Barbecue-Grilled CHICKEN with LAVENDER and THYME

Serves: 4 // Preparation time: 15 minutes
// Marinating time: 1 hour // Cooking time: 30 minutes

INGREDIENTS

8 chicken drumsticks

For the marinade
100ml red wine
4 lavender flowers
finely grated rind of a
    small orange
2 fat cloves of garlic,
    peeled and chopped
2 tsp freshly chopped thyme
½ tsp hot chilli, minced
2 tsp clear honey
2 tbsp olive oil
pinch of salt

METHOD

1. Pour the wine into a stainless steel
   saucepan and reduce over a steady heat
   until about 2 tablespoons remain.

2. Combine the lavender flowers, orange
   rind, garlic, thyme and chilli in a
   pestle and mortar or blender.

3. Add the honey, olive oil, salt
   and reduced red wine.

4. Slash the drumsticks, cover with
   the marinade and leave for at
   least 1 hour, turning once.

5. Preheat a grill or barbecue and
   allow the embers to settle. Cook the
   chicken pieces for 15 minutes until
   cooked through, turning once.

6. Serve with a salad, crusty bread
   and, of course, a glass of red wine.

 Look for the Red Tractor logo when buying your
ingredients to ensure you are buying quality British produce.

Chicken KORMA

Serves: 4 // Preparation time: 20 minutes
// Marinating time: overnight // Cooking time: 30 minutes

INGREDIENTS

4 boneless, skinless
   chicken breasts
150g natural yoghurt
2 garlic cloves, crushed
2 tsp turmeric
40g unsalted butter
1 large onion, sliced
5cm fresh root ginger,
   finely diced
1 tsp chilli powder
1 tsp coriander seeds, crushed
10 whole cloves
1 tsp salt
5cm cinnamon stick
1 tbsp cornflour
150ml single cream
25g unsalted cashew nuts,
   toasted, to garnish

METHOD

1. Score each chicken breast
   with a sharp knife.

2. In a large bowl, mix together the yoghurt,
   garlic and turmeric. Add the chicken and
   coat well in the marinade. Cover and
   leave to marinate overnight in the fridge.

3. Melt the butter in a large frying pan, add
   the onion and cook until soft and browned.

4. Stir in the ginger, chilli powder, coriander
   seeds, cloves, salt and cinnamon
   stick and cook for 2–3 minutes.

5. Add the chicken and its marinade
   and cook on a gentle heat for 20–25
   minutes until the chicken is completely
   cooked. Reduce the heat.

6. Blend the cornflour and cream together
   and stir into the chicken. Reheat very
   gently to prevent the cream from curdling.
   Sprinkle over the cashew nuts to garnish.

7. Serve with rice.

CHICKEN *mousse* with FRESH GARDEN PEAS and TARRAGON

Serves: 4–6 // Preparation time: 15 minutes

INGREDIENTS

100g fresh or frozen peas
225g cooked chicken breasts
juice and rind of 1 small lemon
1 tbsp freshly chopped
    tarragon
3 tbsp mayonnaise
1 tsp Dijon mustard
3 tbsp whipped double cream
salt and freshly ground
    black pepper
red and white chicory
    leaves, to serve

METHOD

1. Cook the peas in boiling water for
   2–3 minutes until tender. Drain and
   refresh under cold running water
   to keep the bright colour. When
   cold, pat dry with kitchen paper.

2. Remove any skin from the chicken
   and discard. Cut the meat into small
   pieces and place in a food processor
   with the lemon rind and juice, tarragon,
   mayonnaise and mustard. Process to
   form a smooth mousse. Add the peas
   and pulse to mix into a mousse but don't
   overwork. Fold in the whipped cream.
   Season to taste. Chill until needed.

3. To serve, place spoonfuls of the mousse
   on to the stalk ends of the chicory
   leaves. Arrange on a serving platter
   and scatter with chopped chives.

TOP TIP This is an ideal recipe to use up any chicken left over from a roast dinner.

MEET THE FARMER

Tim Papworth

Meet Tim Papworth, a fourth-generation farmer in North Norfolk, where his family keeps a mixed agricultural, sheep and cattle farm alongside tenancies and contract farming. His farmhouse keeps a murderous secret...

For Tim, farming brings a love of the seasons and daily challenges on his farm. His abiding hope is that he will leave a better place for his children to take on when they are ready. He has made many friends in the agricultural community and had some wonderful experiences. As well as running his own farm and tenancies, Tim and his family contract farm for 25 landlords with a wide range of different agreements.

"We are a very mixed farm, growing different crops," says Tim. "Here in these recipes, we are showcasing our potatoes – we grow all sorts for chipping, crisping and processing."

Tim's potato varieties include:

- for salads: Exquisa, Esmerelda, Galante, Piccolo Star;
- for crisping: Daisy, Endeavour;
- for chipping: Innovator, Royal, Premiere;
- for processing: Daisy, Rooster.

"We also provide meat from our own sheep and beef cattle to our butcher's shops and meat processing units," he continues.

Tim's daily routine has an early start, getting up at 5.45am for breakfast and a quick scan of the paper. Work starts in earnest with a chat over plans with his business partner, taking calls and replying to emails, talking to staff and checking the cattle, all before 9am. At the peak of the potato harvest, work can go on until late in the evening, so Tim buys the staff a take-away and it's all hands to the pump – or potato harvester! His treat for lunch on a Friday is often fish and chips, although his favourite dish is steak and chips, using Papworth beef and potatoes, of course.

And the farm's murderous secret? William Rush murdered his mother with poisoned cake in Tim's spare bedroom back in 1849. William Rush was one of the last people to be hanged at Norwich prison.

LANCASHIRE
Hotpot

Serves: 4 // Preparation time: 20 minutes // Cooking time: 2 hours 20 minutes

INGREDIENTS

25g plain flour
salt and freshly ground
   black pepper
675g middle or best end of
   neck lamb chops, trimmed
   of visible fat
2 large onions, sliced
2 lamb's kidneys, skinned,
   cored and sliced
675g potatoes, sliced
1 tbsp freshly chopped
   rosemary
25g unsalted butter, melted
425ml lamb stock

METHOD

1. Preheat the oven to 160°C/
   fan 140°C/350°F/gas mark 4.

2. Sift the flour into a shallow dish and
   season well. Add the chops and turn to
   coat evenly in the seasoned flour.

3. Arrange layers of meat, onion, kidney
   and potato in a large, lidded, ovenproof
   casserole dish. Sprinkle each layer with a
   little rosemary and some seasoning and
   finish with a layer of potatoes.

4. Brush the top of the potatoes with the
   melted butter. Pour the stock into the
   casserole dish and cover it tightly with
   a lid. Cook for 1½–2 hours, or until the
   meat is tender.

5. Remove the lid from the casserole and
   cook for an extra 20 minutes to brown
   the potatoes.

TOP TIP
If you don't have a lidded casserole dish, use a regular
ovenproof dish and cover with foil.

SPANISH
Tortilla

Serves: 4 // Preparation time: 15 minutes // Cooking time: 25 minutes

INGREDIENTS

2 tbsp olive oil
2 medium cooked potatoes,
   cut into 1.5–2cm cubes
1 medium red onion, sliced
salt and freshly ground
   black pepper
50g chorizo, cubed
1 chargrilled red pepper from
   a jar, sliced (optional)
4 large free-range eggs

METHOD

1. Heat half the oil in a large frying pan and
   add the potatoes, onion, and plenty of
   seasoning. Cook over a medium heat for
   5 minutes until the potatoes are golden.
   Add the chorizo and red pepper, if using,
   and cook for a couple more minutes.

2. Put the eggs in a bowl with more
   seasoning and beat with a fork.

3. Add the hot vegetables from the pan
   and mix thoroughly. Leave to stand for
   5 minutes.

4. Heat the remaining oil in a 20cm
   non-stick frying pan until very hot and
   pour in the egg mixture. Stir with a fork,
   lifting the middle of the tortilla to let the
   uncooked egg run down into the base.
   Cook over a medium heat for 4–5 minutes
   until the egg is set and the base is golden.

5. Place a large plate over the pan and very
   carefully invert the frying pan to tip the
   tortilla out onto the plate, cooked side
   upwards. Carefully slide it back in to the
   pan to cook the other side. To get the
   traditional cake shape, slide the tortilla
   back into the pan a couple more times
   until the whole thing is golden brown and
   cooked through. Turn onto a plate and
   serve warm or at room temperature.

VENISON
Casserole

Serves: 6 // Preparation time: 5 minutes // Marinate: 24 hours
// Cooking time: 30–45 minutes

INGREDIENTS

900g lean venison, diced
450ml red wine
8 juniper berries
2 fresh bay leaves
2 sprigs fresh thyme
2 tbsp seasoned flour
2–3 tbsp oil
225g shallots
350g celeriac, peeled
  and cut into chunks
3 carrots, peeled and cut
  into chunks
150ml beef stock
4 tbsp redcurrant jelly
fresh thyme to garnish

METHOD

1. Place the venison into a large bowl and
   pour over the red wine. Add the juniper
   berries, bay leaves and thyme. Cover and
   leave to marinate in the fridge for 24 hours.

2. Remove the venison from the
   marinade and pat dry with kitchen
   paper (reserve the marinade). Toss
   the meat in the seasoned flour.

3. Preheat the oven to 160°C/
   fan 140°C/325°F/gas mark 3.

4. Heat the oil in a large flameproof casserole
   dish and sear the venison in batches until
   browned all over, adding a little more oil if
   necessary. Remove with a slotted spoon.

5. Fry the shallots in the casserole for
   2–3 minutes, then stir in the marinade
   and stock and bring to the boil.
   Return the venison to the casserole
   and add the celeriac and carrots.

6. Cover the casserole and cook
   in the oven for 1¾ hours.

7. Stir in the redcurrant jelly and return
   to the oven for a further 30–45 minutes
   until the venison is completely tender.

8. Serve with mashed potato and
   garnish with fresh thyme.

PEAR and Ginger
PARKIN

Serves: 12 // Preparation time: 10 minutes // Cooking time: 1 hour 10 minutes

INGREDIENTS

100g butter
100g treacle
100g golden syrup
250g plain flour
1 tbsp ground mixed spice
2 tsp baking powder
75g light muscovado sugar
250g medium oatmeal
1 large egg, beaten
150ml milk
100g stem ginger,
    finely chopped
2 firm pears, peeled,
    cored and chopped
2 tbsp stem ginger syrup

METHOD

1. Preheat the oven to 170°C/
   fan 150°C/335°F/gas mark 3.

2. Put the butter, treacle and syrup
   in a pan and heat until the butter
   has melted. Cool slightly.

3. Sift the flour, mixed spice and
   baking powder into a large bowl and
   stir in the sugar and oatmeal.

4. Stir the melted mixture into the bowl
   with the egg and milk, and mix well.

5. Fold in nearly all the stem ginger and
   pears, reserving a little for decoration.

6. Spoon the mixture into a greased and
   lined 20cm square cake tin. Level
   the surface and scatter over the rest
   of the ginger and pear pieces.

7. Bake for 1 hour 10 minutes or until
   firm and a skewer inserted into the
   middle of the cake comes out clean.

8. Brush over the syrup and leave to cool.
   When cold, remove from the tin and wrap
   in greaseproof paper. Store in an airtight
   container and leave to mature for
   1–2 weeks.

MEET the FARMER

James Smith

James Smith, managing director of Loddington Farm Ltd, grows a lovely variety of fruit, south of Maidstone and near Laddingford in Kent: known as one of the best fruit basket areas in England.

This farm is a real family affair. James is a fifth generation farmer; his 17 month-old son Theo, together with seven cousins, form the sixth generation, so there are plenty of people to continue the family legacy. His father is still involved and even though he is 76 years old he likes to help out on the farm.

James' sister and cousin also run Blooming Green, a pick your own flower business on the farm, so imagine the flowers in spring – apple, pear, cherry and apricot blossoms cover their orchards on the Greensand Ridge and in the Weald of Kent, alongside flowers for picking. In addition to the Gala, Braeburn, Cox, Bramley, Kentish Kiss and Red Windsor apples, which make up 80% of the business, they also grow Conference pears and asparagus.

Time is at a premium as the farm also closely manages its own transport and cold stores. They pick everything by hand, using workers mostly from Romania, and James has two full-time workers all year round. "Brexit is a major concern for farming for many reasons, including the availability of a reliable, competent workforce," he says. "I worry that our current workers might not be able, or want to come and work here in the future. Not getting the crop picked on time could be the end for most growers so it poses a real threat to our industry."

Although James says farming can be difficult and challenging, he loves producing food, and cherishes the responsibility he has looking after the countryside. During busy harvest days, he rises around 6am to join the 50 staff needed at this time to pick the fruit. James says: "My time is spent seeing that everyone knows what they are doing and has everything they need to do it."

James is proud that they grew the world's heaviest apple in 1997, which was recorded in the Guinness Book of World Records. "It weighed 3lb 11oz, so it was an absolute whopper."

It is little wonder that his favourite dish is blackberry and apple crumble, following his roast beef Sunday lunch.

Apple CRUMBLE

Serves: 4 // Preparation and cooking time: 1 hour 15 minutes

INGREDIENTS

For the filling
1.2kg Bramley apples,
    peeled, cored, and diced
175g caster sugar
100ml water

For the crumble topping
225g plain flour
60g ground almonds
120g soft brown sugar
60g caster sugar
pinch of salt
1 tsp ground cinnamon
160g unsalted butter,
    cold and cubed

METHOD

1. For the filling: preheat the oven to 180°C/
   fan 160°C/350°F/gas mark 4.

2. Combine the apple, sugar, and water in a large,
   heavy-based saucepan. Cover and cook over a
   medium heat, stirring from time to time, for about
   15–20 minutes until the fruit is soft. When ready,
   remove from the heat and let it cool on one side.

3. For the topping: combine the flour, ground almonds,
   brown sugar, caster sugar, salt, and cinnamon
   in a food processor. Pulse briefly to mix.

4. Add the butter and pulse until the mixture
   resembles rough breadcrumbs; it should still be
   rough and textured.

5. Scatter the crumble mixture over a large baking
   tray, spreading it out evenly. Bake for 25–30
   minutes until golden brown and crisp. Remove
   from the oven and let it cool for 5 minutes.

6. Reheat the apple before dividing between bowls.
   Top with the crumble mixture before serving.

  TOP TIP — Did you know Silver Spoon granulated, caster and icing sugar is the only sugar made from 100% British sugar beet? It takes about 4–6 beets to produce one pack of sugar.

Gingerbread CAKE with PEARS

Serves: 8 // Preparation time: 30 minutes // Cooking time: 60 minutes

INGREDIENTS

170g self-raising flour
1 tsp ground ginger
half a level tsp of grated
    nutmeg
half a level tsp of cinnamon
pinch salt
2 eggs, beaten
2 tbsp black treacle
85ml milk
85g butter, softened
145g muscovado sugar

Topping
60g butter
60g muscovado sugar
1–2 pears, peeled and sliced

METHOD

1. Preheat the oven to 180°C/
   fan 160°C/350°F/gas mark 4.

2. Grease and line an 18cm cake tin.

3. Sift the flour, spices and salt into a bowl.

4. Mix the eggs, treacle, milk, butter
   and sugar and beat into the flour.

5. In a separate bowl, cream the butter and
   sugar together.

6. For the topping: spread the mixture
   around the bottom of the cake tin.
   Arrange the pear slices on top.

7. Pour the flour mixture over the pears and
   smooth over.

8. Bake for 45–50 minutes, then stand for
   10 minutes and invert. Serve warm with
   cream or custard.

  TOP TIP Look for the British Lion mark when buying eggs.

MEET the FARMER

Sophie Hope

Sophie Hope has returned to the family farm where they raise chickens.

Sophie Hope, in her early thirties and mother to a 13-month-old son, returned to the family farm in Gloucestershire in 2013, after gaining a degree in natural sciences, spending a year studying for a masters degree at the Royal Agricultural College, and helping at a Suffolk pig farming business.

Alexander & Angell (Farms) Ltd was taken over by the Hope family in the 1970s and is now in its third generation of management. Following both her grandfather and dad, Andrew, who took the farm on in the 70s, she is now beginning to take charge.

The core of the business is poultry and pig farming. "We have 81,000 broiler breeders on three farms," says Sophie. "Broiler breeders are the parent stock of the meat bird you buy, so we have both pullets (female chickens) and cockerels on farm, producing fertile hatching eggs, delivering 12 million broilers a year."

The chicken duties start at 6am, checking for health, feed, water, ventilation, fresh shavings for bedding, and correct weight gain. Any eggs laid on the floor are picked up. Eggs are mainly laid in the dark in nest boxes running down the centre of the barns. These roll onto a conveyor belt, and are collected and packed onto trays in a central control room. For example, on one of their farms housing 24,550 pullets, they produced 22,545 eggs per day, of which 21,890 were hatching eggs (the remainder would have been small, cracked or double yolks). Four weeks later, 19,700 chicks hatched.

Because the farm is so varied, there's always plenty to do, with a mix of outdoor and office work in beautiful surroundings. Sophie loves working for herself with a great team around her. Although learning how to run a large business is hard and daunting, she can't imagine doing anything else and says she feels very lucky to have this opportunity.

"British agriculture is so important and needs to be kept alive. I'm really interested in teaching others about agriculture and showing people what we do," she explains. "I liked participating in Open Farm Sunday – we have a public viewing room on one of our poultry farms."

Her favourite British chicken recipe is a chicken, bacon and mushroom pie.

Great British LARDER

Buy British when it's in abundance
with this seasonal guide.

Food all YEAR ROUND

British meat, eggs and dairy can be bought
throughout the year:
Beef, chicken, turkey, pork, sausage, bacon,
milk, cream, cheese, yoghurt, and eggs.

Some fresh British produce is available almost all year round too:

Apples	Lettuce	Potatoes
Beetroot	Micro leaves	Salad cress
Cabbage	Mushrooms	Salad leaves
Carrots	Onions	Salad potatoes
Cauliflower	Pak choi	Swede
Celeriac	Parsnips	Tomatoes
Chicory	Pea shoots	
Cucumber	Purple sprouting broccoli	

For the full version of Great British Larder visit:
www.nfuonline.com/greatbritishlarder

Winter

BRUSSELS SPROUTS Dec–Feb
BUTTERNUT SQUASH Dec
JERUSALEM ARTICHOKE Dec–Feb
KALE Dec–Feb
LAMB Dec–Jan
LEEKS Dec–Feb
PEARS Dec–Feb
PUMPKINS/SQUASH Dec
RHUBARB Jan–Feb
SPRING GREENS Dec–Feb
TURNIPS Dec–Feb

Spring

ASPARAGUS Apr–May
AUBERGINES May
BROAD BEANS Apr–May
BRUSSELS SPROUTS Mar
CHARD Apr–May
JERUSALEM ARTICHOKE Mar
KALE Mar
LEEKS Mar–May
NEW POTATOES May
PEARS Mar–May
PEPPERS Mar–May
RADISHES Apr–May
RASPBERRIES May
RHUBARB Mar–May
ROCKET Apr–May
SPINACH Mar–May
SPRING GREENS Mar–May
SPRING ONIONS Apr–May
STRAWBERRIES Apr–May
WATERCRESS May

Summer

APRICOTS Jul–Aug	**LAMB** Jul–Aug
ASPARAGUS Jun	**LEEKS** Aug
AUBERGINES Jun–Aug	**MARROWS** Jul–Aug
BLACKBERRIES Jun–Aug	**NEW POTATOES** Jun–Aug
BLACKCURRANTS Jun–Aug	**PEAS** Jun–Aug
BLUEBERRIES Jun–Aug	**PEPPERS** Jun–Aug
BROCCOLI Jun–Aug	**PLUMS** Jul–Aug
BRUSSELS SPROUTS Aug	**RADISHES** Jun–Aug
BROAD BEANS Jun–Aug	**RASPBERRIES** Jun–Aug
CELERY Jun–Aug	**REDCURRANTS** Jul–Aug
CHARD Jun–Aug	**RHUBARB** Jun–Aug
CHERRIES Jun–Aug	**ROCKET** Jun–Aug
COURGETTES Jun–Aug	**RUNNER BEANS** Jul–Aug
DWARF BEANS Jul–Aug	**SPINACH** Jun–Aug
FENNEL Jun–Aug	**SPRING ONIONS** Jun–Aug
FLAT BEANS Jul–Aug	**STRAWBERRIES** Jun–Aug
GARLIC Jun–Aug	**SUGAR SNAP PEAS** Jun–Aug
GLOBE ARTICHOKE Jun–Aug	**SWEETCORN** Jul–Aug
GOOSEBERRIES Jun–Aug	**TURNIPS** Jun–Aug
KALE Jun–Aug	**WATERCRESS** Jun–Aug

Autumn

APRICOTS Sept

AUBERGINES Sept–Oct

BLACKBERRIES Sept–Nov

BLUEBERRIES Sept

BROAD BEANS Sept–Oct

BROCCOLI Sept–Nov

BRUSSELS SPROUTS Sept–Nov

BUTTERNUT SQUASH Sept–Nov

CELERY Sept–Oct

CHARD Sept–Nov

COURGETTES Sept–Oct

DWARF BEANS Sept–Oct

FENNEL Sept–Nov

FLAT BEANS Sept

GARLIC Sept

GLOBE ARTICHOKE Sept–Nov

KALE Sept–Nov

LAMB Sept–Nov

LEEKS Sept–Nov

MARROWS Sept–Nov

NEW POTATOES Sept–Oct

PEARS Sept–Nov

PEAS Sept

PEPPERS Sept–Nov

PLUMS Sept–Oct

PUMPKINS/SQUASH Sept–Nov

RADISHES Sept–Oct

RASPBERRIES Sept–Nov

RHUBARB Sept–Oct

ROCKET Sept–Oct

RUNNER BEANS Sept–Oct

SPINACH Sept–Nov

SPRING GREENS Nov

SPRING ONIONS Sept–Oct

STRAWBERRIES Sept–Nov

SWEETCORN Sept–Nov

TURNIPS Sept–Nov

WATERCRESS Sept–Oct

RED TRACTOR

Quality, British food. You expect it and farmers deliver it. If you want to know that the food you eat has been reared and grown to some of the highest standards of animal welfare and environmental protection in the world, look no further than the Red Tractor logo on pack.

Red Tractor and the British food and farming community work together to ensure the food on your plate has been independently inspected and checked along each and every step of the way. From field to packing house, from transporter to retailer, you can trust the Red Tractor. Since the 1990s, the Red Tractor food scheme has ensured that all stages in the food production and supply chain are regularly checked by independent experts to put the best of British food on your plate.

Now, all major UK supermarkets use the Red Tractor standards as the basis for their UK-sourced food, with the Red Tractor logo on more than £12 billion-worth of food and drink every year.

More than 2,000 food service companies throughout the UK also proudly display the Red Tractor logo including giants such as KFC, Nandos and Mitchells & Butlers.

And the Red Tractor's goal is to get their stamp of approval on even more products as chairman Jim Mosely explains:

"We have worked hard with thousands of farmers over the years to develop a really robust set of standards which are reviewed regularly. Our farmers belong to Red Tractor

Farm Assurance Schemes with standards of good agricultural practice covering food safety, protection from pollution and — for livestock — animal health and welfare.

"British farmers are hugely passionate about their role as custodians of the countryside, hugely proud of their animal welfare and know intrinsically what it takes to produce quality, wholesome foods.

"As well as fresh meat and vegetables carrying the Red Tractor logo, the seal of approval is carried on ready-made products to show their main ingredients are produced to the highest of standards, helping shoppers to navigate what can be complex and complicated food labels.

"But it is equally important to have the whole of the supply chain included so the Red Tractor assurance scheme also ensures food companies conform to these high standards and that food is clearly labelled, proving it has come from Red Tractor assured supply chains.

"Red Tractor, working with organisations such as the NFU, encourages customers to choose assured products and is the only scheme that offers full traceability of products, from farm to pack. It is also one of the best ways people can back British farming by looking out for and buying Red Tractor food and drink."

Deluxe

BRITISH
ARAGUS TIPS

SELECTED FOR THEIR SWEET FLAVOUR

re:
08/05/2015
W632(81) E521

who shar

pork chops

price	E per
4.00	7

approx. cooking time
grill
20-28 mins

Fresh semi- skimmed milk.
Pasteurised, homogenised,
semi- skimmed milk.

568 ml
1 pint

Index

ACKNOWLEDGEMENTS

The National Farmers' Union would like to thank the following for the use of recipes and photographs

The Women's Institute

Cream of broad bean soup. From *The WI Centenary Cookbook* by Mary Gwynn (Ebury 2015) p.148. Original recipe from the WI Home Skills book *Dinner Parties* in 1979. Photograph by Jan Baldwin

Green bean risotto. From the WI book *Cooking from the Garden* by Sara Lewis (Simon & Schuster, 2012) p.32. Photograph by William Shaw

Steak and chermoula salad. From the WI book *Cooking from the Garden* by Sara Lewis (Simon & Schuster, 2012) p.34. Photograph by William Shaw

Beef wellington. From *The WI Centenary Cookbook* by Mary Gwynn (Ebury 2015) p.168. Original recipe in the WI's *Home and Country* magazine in 1993. Photograph by Jan Baldwin

Tomato tarte tatin. From the WI book *Traditional Favourites* (Simon & Schuster 2012) p.58. Original recipe from 2002 title *Best Kept Secrets of the Women's Institute*. Photograph by William Shaw

Tomato and pepper penne. From the WI book *Cooking from the Garden* by Sara Lewis (Simon & Schuster, 2012) p.56. Photograph by William Shaw

Baked eggs with spinach. From *The WI Centenary Cookbook* by Mary Gwynn (Ebury 2015) p.116. Original Recipe by Surrey Federation Chairman Joan Lash in her book *The Surrey Chicken* published in 1965. Photograph by Jan Baldwin

Barbeque grilled chicken with lavender and thyme. From *The WI Centenary Cookbook* by Mary Gwynn (Ebury 2015) p.178. Original Recipe from the *Feasts from the Vineyard* section in *Home and Country* Magazine in 1998. Photograph by Jan Baldwin

Chicken korma. From the WI book *One pot dishes* (Simon & Schuster 2012) p.40. Original Recipe from 2002 title *Best Kept Secrets of the Women's Institute*. Photograph by William Shaw

Chicken mousse with fresh peas and tarragon. From *The WI Centenary Cookbook* by Mary Gwynn (Ebury 2015) p.48. Original Recipe by H Pearl Adam in *Home and Country* in 1930. Photograph by Jan Baldwin

Lancashire hot pot. From the WI book *One pot dishes* (Simon & Schuster 2012) p.70. Original Recipe from 2002 title *Best Kept Secrets of the Women's Institute*. Photograph by William Shaw

Spanish tortilla. From *The WI Centenary Cookbook* by Mary Gwynn (Ebury 2015) p.92. Original Recipe by in the WI's *Home and Country* magazine in 1954. Photograph by Jan Baldwin

Artwork Jan Baldwin
From *The WI Cookbook*
by Mary Gwynn
Published by Ebury Press Reprinted by permission of The Random House Group Limited
© 2015

AHDB

Lovepotatoes.co.uk for the one pot pork and potato chilli and sausage and potato cassoulet recipes

Simplybeefandlamb.co.uk for the roast sirloin of beef with chestnut and chive butter, warm lamb and noodle salad and the individual lamb wellingtons recipes

Ladies in Beef
Simplybeefandlamb.co.uk for the image and recipe for the beef and chutney toasties

British Growers Association

britishcarrots.co.uk for the parsnip and ginger soup, layered parsnip and Lancashire bake, warm beef with winter vegetable salad and caramelised parsnip and leek recipes

britishleeks.co.uk for the leek and Stilton soup and leek and pear tart recipes

britishonions.co.uk for the caramelised onion and cheese soufflé

enjoyasparagus.com for the cream of asparagus soup with poached egg

loveyourgreens.co.uk for the creamed Brussels sprouts and nutmeg, the roasted broccoli and cauliflower with lemon and garlic and the cauliflower and cheese soup recipes

britishtomatoes.co.uk for the aromatic stuffed tomatoes recipe

British Summer Fruits
seasonalberries.co.uk for the pork, cherry and pistachio terrine, strawberry trifle with Pimms and the strawberry and raspberry Eton mess recipes

The Emsworth Cookery School Ltd
emsworthcookeryschool.co.uk who kindly provided the recipe for Tangmere Airfield Nurseries

Lovebeetroot.co.uk
for the citrus and baby beetroot kale salad recipe

Love the Crunch Campaign
lovethecrunch.com for the spring onion and feta frittata

Rosemary Moon
rosemarymoon.com for duck with hot chillies, cool peppers and apple raita recipe, who kindly provided the recipe and image for Tangmere Airfield Nurseries. For more information on Tangmere, visit: tangmere.co.uk

Yes peas!
www.peas.org for the green pea and pancetta soup

Additional recipes
© StockFood, The Food Media Agency